THe POLiTiCaL PULPIT

THE POLITICAL PULPIT

by Roderick P. Hart

The Purdue University Press
West Lafayette, Indiana
1977

Church and State - United States
United States - Religion - 1945-

©1977 by the Purdue Research Foundation
Library of Congress Catalog Number 76-12290
International Standard Book Numbers
Clothbound edition, 0-911198-44-X
Paperbound edition, 0-911198-45-8
Printed in the United States of America

To

James Clarke
Jay Savereid
Carroll Arnold
    Scholars and gentle persons all

CONTENTS

ACKNOWLEDGMENTS

Even at the risk of rendering perfectly innocent persons guilty via their kind associations, I simply must thank certain individuals for helping me in this project. Central among them are:

Professors Richard Gregg and Conrad Cherry of the Pennsylvania State University, Professor Kathleen Jamieson of the University of Maryland, and Professor Lawrence Rosenfield of Hunter College. Without them, I surely would have committed all manner of theoretical mayhem. That I may still have managed to do so is, of course, my fault, not theirs.

Professor Charles Stewart of Purdue University, a colleague and friend who encouraged me greatly throughout the project.

The Purdue Research Foundation, which saw fit to provide me with research monies during the initial stages of this study.

Doctoral students Carol Jablonski, Michael Hyde, and James Walsh, who assisted me in matters both practical and theoretical.

Diana Cable and Jan Terrell, whose timely and competent ministrations offset the monstrous indignities which my Smith-Corona portable insisted on making.

Frank Ruggirello, whose reaction to this project provided me with much needed motivation.

Finally, and most centrally, Peggy, Chris, and Kate—three very special people who stand as a collective reason for doing this sort of thing.

PRELUDE

Let us go forward, firm in our faith, steadfast in our purpose, cautious of the dangers; but sustained by our confidence in the will of God and the promise of man.

(Richard Nixon, first inaugural address, January 20, 1969)

To have served in this office is to have felt a very personal sense of kinship with each and every American. In leaving it, I do so with this prayer: May God's grace be with you in all the days ahead.

(Richard Nixon, resignation speech, August 8, 1974)

Thus began, and ended, an American presidency—a presidency of hope and despair, of success and failure, of passion, of vitriol, and finally, of concession. But rhetorically speaking, it appears that Richard Nixon's presidency was one "of God."

The cynic, of course, would dismiss the religious themes in presidential speeches as matters of little moment—as constituting nothing more than ritualistic homage being paid by expedient politicians to a religion-conscious electorate. As sociologist Robert Bellah notes, however, every American president has imbedded such religious waxings and wanings into his most hallowed addresses. Indeed, Bellah argues that such religion-filled political rhetoric is perhaps the clearest and most virulent expression of our

1

national ideals and values, of a unique and very American consensus, of an "American civil religion."

In his much-touted essay written in 1967,[1] Bellah eloquently crystalized a conception which had previously, but obliquely, been referred to by a number of scholars. Put briefly, Bellah suggested that the ceremonial remarks of American presidents universally contain allusions to our moral and political ideals as a country and to our national understanding of God and the American Way. Subsequent commentaries made on Bellah's essay have, by and large, agreed with his central contentions: (1) that presidential pronouncements are reliable indicators of powerful religious yearnings among the American people; (2) that such presidential statements can best be interpreted as signifying the existence of as "national religion" among Americans; and (3) that attendant to such a "religion" are potentially salutatory implications for us as a nation of citizen-believers.

Because Bellah based many of his contentions on phenomena he had observed in presidential speeches, the rhetorical scholar appears to be uniquely equipped to investigate the assumptions, conclusions, and implications of Bellah's American civil religion. Thus, when venturing into the inadequately charted rhetorical waters of civil religion in this essay, I shall operate on the basis of two fundamental assumptions: (1) that the American civil religion is, in essence, a complex network of richly symbolic activities and (2) that the peculiar intellectual tastes and special abilities of the rhetorical analyst allow him or her to appropriate the nature of civic piety in a rather direct manner. Because both suppositions underlie all of the remarks to be made in this essay, I shall examine each of them briefly.

To the best of my knowledge, no scholar or popular commentator has yet completely confused Bellah's "civil" religion with "real" religion. Rather, all seem to agree that civil religion constitutes what Kenneth Burke[2] might call a system of symbolic, dramatic action and that its motivating force emanates from man's need for those hagiographic elements so crucial in a nation's emotional life. Such symbolic action, Burke might argue, derives equally from the saying as from the said, as much from the pageantry of the inaugural activities as from the specifics of the address itself. "To the average man," claims rhetorical scholar Herbert Simons, "politics is a 'spectator sport' on which he can project his desires, fears, and his wishes. The primary requirement of the politician is not that he bestow tangible benefits but that he take dramatic action."[3] Throughout this essay, therefore, I shall follow the symbolic action of civil religion, attempting at each step along the way to avoid reifying that most intangible of human stuff—symbolization.

Despite the considerable amount of scholarship which has been devoted to civil-religious matters, nowhere have I found writers taking careful rhetorical measures of such symbolic interplay. Most commentators have discussed only the macro-sociological or macro-theological dimensions of civil religion, thus allowing the specific verbal details of civic piety to go unexamined. Such a state of affairs is perplexing. After all, anthropologists like Johannes Fabian have claimed that *"objectivity* in anthropological investigations is attained by examining a context of communicative interaction through the one medium which represents and constitutes such a context: *language,"*[4] and sociologist Andrew Greeley has asserted that "what is required in dealing with civil religion is not attack or defense but hermeneutics."[5] Throughout the development of this essay, I shall hearken faithfully to such calls for hard-nosed rhetorical analysis. But I shall do so not in an attempt to put the anthropologists' and sociologists' houses in order, but because a rhetorical perspective on human symbolic activities makes for insight of a very special sort, as has been ably suggested by Richard Gregg:

> We [humans] construct and interpret our reality, evaluate it, and adopt strategies for taking action by creating, modifying and maintaining symbols which function rhetorically. Now, human ingenuity is a marvelous thing; human symbolic accomplishment cannot always be captured within the interaction matrices employed by sociologists, the often simplified belief structures perceived by religionists, or the rational behavior models comforting to many historians. What is so often missed is the mixture of fantasy and myth, purpose and accident, and dramatistic play, all of which mask or manifest a variety of intentions that comprise what Kenneth Burke calls the human barnyard. It is this complex realm of symbolic maneuvering that the rhetorical scholar seeks to understand. . . .[6]

The approach to be taken here will thus be a rhetorical one. But what does it mean—pragmatically—to adopt a rhetorical point of view? How is it that one approaches a study rhetorically?

Wherein lies the value of a rhetorical perspective of human activity?

Among many other things, the rhetorical viewpoint implies that:

1. Discourse of a public sort constitutes the scholar's focal point of concern;
2. The processes of creating discourse and the popular responses made to such discourse are seen as significant objects of intellectual inquiry;
3. The rhetorical scholar seeks to understand the interaction between cultural values and the discourse through which such feelings are publicly conveyed;
4. The themes, arguments, structures, and language which make up public communications are viewed as significant only insofar as they can be carefully elucidated and intelligently explained;
5. Consideration is accorded the ethical worth of a body of rhetoric only after the socio-symbolic aspects of such phenomena have been fully explicated.[7]

Because it is so concerned, the rhetorical approach differs considerably from the theological, historical, and sociological perspectives by which the American civil religion has been viewed heretofore. Still, this essay has a significant interdisciplinary debt to pay. Like the theologian, I shall be interested in the ethical implications of civil-religious discourse if and when such matters become relevant to the public at large. Like the historian, I shall examine antecedent forms of civic piety insofar as they bear relevance to the current rhetorical scene in America. Like the sociologist, I shall seek to understand social values and cultural continuities to the extent that such values and norms are reflected in popular discourse. Thus, my examination of civil religion in America will be singular in its scholarly focus yet, at the same time, indebted to (and hopefully refreshed by) diverse academic viewpoints.

As we move along in this study, I hope we shall begin to see one of the most commonplace features of the American experience. We shall observe numerous American presidents hurriedly ordering their aides to find an appropriate amount of "God stuff" with which to invigorate their upcoming address to the ladies of Pocatello. We shall notice various and sundry

American prelates vying with one another for the privilege of offering the benediction at political gatherings from Washington to Waukesha. We shall listen to Dwight D. Eisenhower, a universal choice for first deacon in our national congregation, as he opines with a generous amount of civic piety: "Our government makes no sense unless it is founded in a deeply felt religious faith, and I don't care what it is."[8]

If one views such curiosities with a completely jaundiced eye, however, one would misunderstand a powerful and ubiquitous force in American political and religious life. To dismiss such religion-larded political speeches as just so much electioneering chicanery is to allow polemics to obstruct our understanding of an unquestionable and powerful reality. On the other hand, if one were to act prematurely as an apologist for our national cult-making, one would be forsaking the objectivity, or consciousness of subjectivity, necessary for understanding fully the political, religious, and politico-religious dimensions of the American nation. In short, to argue, as Hutchinson has, that every politician who kneels in public prayer can be rightly suspected of having one eye opened toward a press camera, is to say far too little.[9] On the other hand, to view the rhetorical interlacings of religion and politics as forces which constitute the "authentic American affirmation," as has the Reverend Joseph Costanzo,[10] is to engage in a bit too much Jesuit exuberance.

Thus, in the pages that follow, I shall strive to examine dispassionately a wide array of civil-religious discourse, some of which is urbane, other of which is bombastic. More specifically, I shall progress as follows when reexamining the story of American civic piety. First, I shall seek to explain the scope and influence of civic piety, distinguishing between "official" and "unofficial" varieties of religio-political discourse and noting briefly what seems to be a veritable panorama of powerful, symbolic phenomena. Next, I shall concern myself with the various theoretical models which have been used to explain the influence and ubiquity of civic piety in America, after which I shall propose what seems to me to be a happier method for understanding conceptually such rhetorical activities. Finally, I shall present what I feel to be the primary contribution of this essay—an examination of the generically distinctive qualities of religio-political speechmaking.

When inspecting such matters of scope, nature, and rhetorical manifestation, we shall be observing—for good or ill—the American people. We shall not see them as might a psychoanalyst, for our perspective will be a public one. Yet we may see parts of them that the psychoanalyst, or an army of psychoanalysts, could not. For we shall see them in their most "obvious" ways of being a people. We shall watch them spend hundreds of thousands of dollars on bicentennial celebrations which honor America's religious heritage. We shall see them attend, by the thousands upon thousands, ceremonies presided over by heaven-gazing prelates and by appropriately bowing heads of state. We shall see, too, the scoffing, sometimes angry, dissidents—those who would have us keep our religion and our politics separated both existentially and rhetorically. Yet in all of our "seeing," we shall attempt to announce and interpret, not to denounce or dismiss, no matter what we may feel about Elmer Davis's characterization of the rhetoric of the American civil religion: "The greatest demonstration of the religious character of this administration came on July Fourth, which the President told us all to spend as a day of penance and prayer. Then he himself caught four fish in the morning, played eighteen holes of golf in the afternoon, and spent the evening at the bridge table."[11]

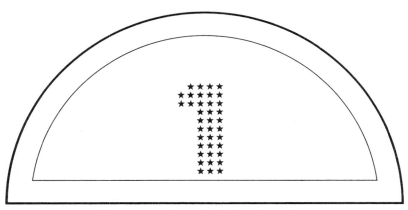

Rhetorical Varieties
of Civic Piety in America

For the jealous viewers in the northern portions of the United States, it appeared to be an ideal evening for a football game. The lights of the stadium burned brightly, as had the southern sun just hours before. The teams, Penn State and L.S.U., were among the best in the nation, a fitting gladiatorial contest with which to terminate another season of college football. The year was just barely 1974, many of the sellout New Year's Day crowd still nursing the bacchanalian wounds suffered the night before. The half-time show was gang-busters.

Seemingly no expense had been spared to provide for home viewers and stadium crowd alike a stirring, emotional half-time extravaganza. The show was all of America on a small scale. The bands marched smartly; the "Stars and Stripes" production number was breathtaking; a clean-cut, young group of singers called the New Directions sang the national anthem with gusto; and the Reverend Billy Bright gave the invocation. The theme of the Reverend Bright's address was a familiar one—that of returning the American nation to its proper Christian heritage. To all but the most wary observer, the Orange Bowl game of January 1, 1974, was a proper affirmation of what the then president would call "what's right with America."

The Orange Bowl, of course, is located in Miami, a city known, among other things, for its sizable Jewish population. Some might find it strange that the national head of the Campus Crusade for Christ was selected for such a rhetorical plum in a city known for its opulence and delicatessens. And yet, to many there was something terribly appropriate about the affair, something traditional, something American. The fact that few eyebrows were raised at the "religious curiosities" seemed to attest to this. It was as if sectarian religious impulses had been set aside on this evening in Miami—set aside for football and the national anthem. It was almost as if, on New Year's Day at least, there was no Jewish or Christian God, only an American God.

In the pages to follow, I shall attempt to explain why Reverend Bright's rhetoric was received as it was, why his sermon was viewed as being so typically American, and why such an invocation was called for at all by the Orange Bowl promoters. I shall point out why, no matter what the radical theologians may contend, God is very much alive in these United States. God dead? In America? No! shouts every American Legion chaplain, every ward-heeler and back-room politico, every country and city parson, every U.S. ambassador to the Vatican, every *Pro Deo Pro Patria* scholarship winner, every star-spangled sermonette, . . . and every Billy Bright in every Orange Bowl.

American Civic Piety: Its Prevalence

Presidential Piety

Ever since Robert Bellah directed our attention to what he termed (in Rousseauian fashion) the "American civil religion," commentary about his analysis has abated not a whit. While very few scholars have questioned the fact that Bellah isolated a significant phenomenon for analysis, many were antagonistic to (or nonplussed by) one of Bellah's conclusions: that the American civil religion has potentially salutary implications for the people of the United States. Michael Novak, for example, argues that this national faith of ours is jingoistic, too culturally self-conscious, and yet not conscious enough of its own moral failings.[1] According to Conrad Cherry, other commentators have accused this "religion" of being theologically naive, sentimentally pious, and idolatrously chauvinistic.[2] Perhaps the most strident attack has been launched by those who see presidential piety and ecclesiastical fawning as evidence of the meanest sort of political bed-fellowing. As George Gordon notes: "A president is . . . free to take his oath of office *sans* Bible and not to mention of God if he so desires, but none has yet had the nerve, or inclination, or both. More significant, perhaps, . . . is the fact that few politicians, no matter how cynical or skeptical of religion they personally are, will end a major political address without a prayer. . . ."[3]

Cavil though we might at this American civil religion of ours, few of us have reason to doubt the significance of the phenomenon Bellah discovered. What Bellah saw in presidential inaugurals was noteworthy: every president since the time of Washington publicly requested or acknowledged help from God for the American people. Taken collectively, Bellah argues, such entreaties reflect what we as a nation find to be most important, to be most right, to be most true. An American president thus becomes, according to Novak, "a priest, a prophet, and a king," a political prelate who reveres this nation's "holy calendar, its sacred cities and monuments and pilgrimages, its consecrated mounds and fields."[4] Thus, when an American president is inaugurated, he is also ordained. According to Robert Alley, Harry Truman carried out his duties as high priest of the American civil religion as competently as any other president:

> In all his actions Mr. Truman had a unique way of injecting religion into policy. From the earliest period of his administration he had requested prayer for his office. He was a member of the First Baptist Church of Washington which he attended on occasion, but it is probably stretching the point to say he attended with "unfailing regularity." He did receive the praise of the religious press when he attended Sunday School in 1947. In a typical overstatement he was acclaimed for setting a good example for all citizens to follow.[5]

Why, one might ask, does the press take pains to offer such "overstatements" and why are such overstatements "typical?" The answer to such questions appears to be "deeply rooted in the American conscience," to borrow a phrase from the scriptures of the American civil religion.

According to Herberg, there are three central components of the American Way of Life, and these beliefs intertwine to make religious pronouncements by American presidents mandatory. Such tenets include belief in God, belief in religion, and belief in the three-faith system (Protestant, Catholic, and Jewish).[6] No American president, it would seem, has the rhetorical option of refusing to pay sufficient and regular homage to such fundamental aspects of our civil religion or of not embellishing such themes. Especially in their public rhetoric, American chief executives must, time and time again, remind themselves and the American people of their triune obligations to God, to country, and to God-and-country. As Billy Graham has remarked, every president has "left the presidency with a very deep religious faith."[7] Indeed, with Thanksgiving proclamations, Christmas messages, prayer breakfasts, congressional invocations, convention benedictions, and the like, such a set of conditions may well have resulted from a rhetorical hangover.

National Piety

The president, of course, is only the central figure in this American civil religion of ours. All Americans have the possibility (according to some, the obligation) of participating regularly and vocally in our national religious ceremonies. During the 1976 bicentennial celebration, for example, Religion in American Life, a national clearinghouse for religious advertising, spent $25 million on an advertising campaign which focused largely on the First Amendment (which guarantees freedom of religion).[8] The program resulted in the dissemination of some 4000 roadside posters, 3.25 million lines of newspaper print, 98,000 car cards on buses, trains, and subways, and a campaign in the electronic media which reached (via repeated exposure) some 1.5 billion home viewers.[9] When such a campaign was coupled with those launched by groups such as the Knights of Columbus, the Volunteers of America, the Exchange Clubs of America, the American Legion, the Catholic War Veterans, and literally thousands of similar groups, the 1976 bicentennial celebrations provided a veritable field day for renewed worship in the American tabernacle of nationhood.

But we would be missing the ubiquitous and far-reaching importance of this national cult were we to focus solely on the grand and unabashedly public means by which we preach our American civil religion. Take, for example, the case of Mary Lou Kierswetter, a Munster, Indiana, housewife who possesses bountiful nationalistic zeal. For a number of years, Ms. Kierswetter directed a campaign to encourage every person living on U.S. 41 (a highway which traverses eight states and runs for some three thousand miles) to fly the American flag regularly. When asked to explain the motivating force which sustained her during her admittedly arduous campaign, Ms. Kierswetter remarked: "If we didn't keep this great nation free it would be sacrilegious. . . . God gave it to us—it's our responsibility to keep it free as He meant it to be."[10]

Organized religion, too, is an equal partner in the preservation and proclamation of our national religious self-understanding. Hardly a day goes by that some religious gathering does not explicitly and forthrightly pay its dues to the nation which has glorified in the religious diversity of its people. Every "mainstream" religious denomination in the United States planned extensive and expensive bicentennial campaigns and ceremonials in every urban, suburban, and rural nook and cranny. The Interchurch Center even established a separate, New York City-based national headquarters (Project F.O.R.W.A.R.D. '76) for the bicentennial celebration, funded it generously, and charged it with retelling the story of America's peculiar sort of tolerance for public professions of religion by presidents and political paupers alike. As Herbert Schneider has said:

> Religion is a pervasive institution. It gets mixed up with education,
> medicine, politics, business, art—there is nothing free from its grasp
> and grasping. All efforts to fence off certain areas of life from which
> the churches must "keep out" have been as futile as similar
> efforts to curtail government or science. Anything can be done
> religiously, and nothing is safe from eccleiastical concern.
> Gone are the days when the salvation of the soul was a distinct
> and separate business. The separation of church and state
> does not separate religion and politics, any more than the
> separation of school and theater separates education and art.[11]

Political Piety: Its Immutability

Such civil-religious goings-on are hardly twentieth-century inventions. The public rhetorical linkings of God and Caesar are older than America itself. Even the novice student of American history is well aware of the pains the American people have taken to surround their political sayings with things divine. Myriad examples of such interlacings abound:

— The Mayflower Compact, authored by forty-one solitary
    pilgrims in 1620, is replete with numerous references to the
    Deity.

— Election sermons, popular vehicles for promulgating American independence in the seventeenth century, are viewed by many historians as constituting one of our first attempts at fashioning a "civil religion."

— Fast and Thanksgiving sermons in the eighteenth century can be viewed as ranking "almost on a par with newspapers, pamphlets, and quasi-legal organizations as mainstays of the war of words which preceded and accompanied the American Revolution."[12]

— In the early years of the republic, "the anniversary of independence was a solemn, quasi-religious ceremonial . . . a prayer was spoken, a hymn or ode sung, the Declaration was read, the oration delivered, another hymn or ode was sung, and prayer closed the ritual."[13]

— The public fasts held during the War of 1812 "showed that the religion and politics of Americans were too closely related to be studied separately."[14]

— In 1861 the words "In God We Trust" were added to our coinage, a practice inspired by the Reverend M. R. Watkinson of Ridleyville, Pennsylvania.

Additionally, we as a nation have fashioned our national anthems, insisted that our presidents take their oaths of office on the Bible, established Capitol prayer rooms, proclaimed national days of prayer, brandished federal banners in our churches, and talked, talked, talked . . . of God's special love for America, of America's unique responsibility to God, of a New Israel and a Chosen People, of rededicating ourselves to the principles of basic, Christian Americanism, and so on.

According to many observers, the 1950s was an especially curious time in the history of the American civil religion. These were the glory days of Billy Graham, Norman Vincent Peale, Fulton Sheen, anti-Communist crusades, McCarthyism, Korea, and the Cold War. But most important, it was a time during which a full 62 percent of the American people professed church membership, and when only one of ninety-five senators in the Eighty-third Congress reported no religious affiliation.[15] In short, the 1950s was a period of unparalleled rhetorical escalating of the American civil religion.

Official Civic Piety: Its Power

Although many commentators have questioned the moral and theological worth of the rhetoric surrounding this "national religion" of ours, the most devastating attack (with regard to its worth as a viable theoretical construct) has been issued by detractors who view the quasi-religious remarks of American politicians as being "mere ceremony," implying that no "real" existential implications inhere in such pronouncements. "There is legal separation of church and state," such persons argue, "and there are no tangible punishments inflicted upon those who would refuse to engage in such rhetorical forms of civic piety, nor are there palpable rewards for so behaving."

Existential Influence
Objections to such a line of reasoning may take at least three forms: legal, political, and psychological. For example, the rhetoric of religion-conscious public officials can be viewed as an oblique sort of legal precedent—a rather pronounced existential implication of our national religion:

> Government proclamations of days of thanksgiving and occasionally prayer are another illustration of ceremonial acts of government which are of slight intrinsic significance but are of great importance in the use to which they are put as precedents to justify far more substantial encroachments of government on religious affairs or religion on government affairs.[16]

Secondly, of course, the American people often use religious criteria when inspecting the rhetoric of those who would presume to lead them politically. As Cohn relates:

> That summer [1952], too, many letters came to Springfield, Illinois, denouncing Governor Stevenson as an "atheist." His offense against God is that he is a Unitarian. . . . As the campaign progressed, another deadly charge was hurled against him. Letter writers convicted him— naturally without trial—upon a different ground. It was that he did not mention God in every speech he made: a failure that indicated he was not only an atheist but also close to "godless Communism."[17]

A less obvious, but equally potent result of this admixture of religion and politics has been pointed out recently by David

Easton and Robert Hess. When studying the political worlds of children, Easton and Hess came upon the rather curious finding that:

> . . . not only do many children associate the sanctity and awe of religion with the political community, but to ages 9 or 10 they sometimes have considerable difficulty in disentangling God and country. . . . The fact that as the child grows older he may be able to sort out the religious from the political setting much more clearly and restrict the pledge to a political meaning, need not thereby weaken this bond. The initial and early intermingling of potent religious sentiment with political community has by that time probably created a tie difficult to dissolve.[18]

In the non-rhetorical dimension of church-state relations, of course, there is an equally long list of very real, very pervasive intertwinings of God and government: elaborate, compulsory sabbath laws, public money to support military and congressional chaplains, required schooling for even Amish and Mennonite children. The list seems endless. To dismiss lightly, therefore, the rhetoric associated with the American civil religion would be to dally unadvisedly with a legally, politically, and psychologically compelling phenomenon.

Symbolic Influence

A second major dimension penetrating our national religion is the symbolic. Kendall and Carey, for example, present a tolerably exhaustive taxonomy of "basic American symbology," and find religious themes to be an ubiquitous part of each major, distinctly American tradition constituting our national experience.[19] In Kenneth Burke's terms, the theological wraps itself around the public consciousness by becoming a "collective poem" which undergirds civil institutions and civil polities.[20] Other writers regard the shimmering religious patina of our political institutions as quite utilitarian and essential to their survival. As Gordon notes: "As far as the author recalls, in fact, no political, social or psychological deterministic stance has yet been evolved which, in its application to groups of people, does not generate a metaphysic— or, to be more specific, does not deal eventually in spiritual and religious-ceremonial matters that usually become central to its own welfare, and, by extension, the welfare of the people at large."[21]

In a relatively straightforward manner, then, religion provides a wealth of symbolic force for governments and political leaders who choose to associate themselves with such forces. Were such powerful, symbolic wellsprings not associated with our religious-political interplay, how could we account for the fact that *Time* magazine found it newsworthy to note that Richard Nixon held thirty-seven Sunday services during his first term but only four during his second?[22] How could we understand the powerful wallop packed by Norman Vincent Peale when he tells his admirers of young Pastor Peter Muhlenberg ending his revolutionary era sermon with: "In the language of the Holy Writ, there is a time for all things. There is a time to preach and a time to fight: and now is the time to fight!"?[23] Or how could we explain the actions of the citizens' group described below, were we not to reckon fully with the symbolic force of the national religion?

> They called themselves the National Citizens' Committee for Fairness to the Presidency, and they assembled 1,400 strong in Washington last week to challenge what their improbable leader—a Taunton, Mass., rabbi named Baruch Korff—called "the lynching psychosis" in Congress and the media. They waved posters and flew flags; they pinned on chrome buttons that said SUPPORT THE PRESIDENCY; they roared and booed and shook their fists as speaker after speaker denounced the press as a pack of wolves or worse. And when the man they had come to rescue appeared briefly before them vowing that he would not leave until his appointment time in 1977, the room fairly rang with their chanting: "God bless Nixon! God bless Nixon! God bless Nixon!"[24]

One of the clearest summary statements of the dramatic, symbolic importance of civil-religious rhetoric is provided by Michael Novak. In *Choosing Our King,* he declares that the question is not whether we shall have a civil religion, but rather what kind of religion it is to be. He goes on to state:

> There are those who despise the notion of a civil religion, out of fear that symbols of transcendence will be perverted to the uses of the state. Whether we like or dislike the notion, however, every national state generates a civil religion. For a state is not solely a pragmatic, administrative agency. The chief officers of the state perform priestly and prophetic roles, conduct huge public liturgies, constantly reinterpret the nation's fundamental documents and traditions, furnish the central terms of public discourse.[25]

Although we have separated for analysis the existential import of civil-religious rhetoric from its symbolic significance, we must remember that the twain do indeed meet. Consider, for example, the case of Ms. Carol Feraci, who was, in 1972, a thirty-year-old registered alien from Toronto, Canada, and a member of Ray Conniff's singing troupe. When the Conniff group appeared at the White House in January 1972, Ms. Feraci improvised a sermon of her own, one directed at that stalwart civil religionist and then president, Richard Nixon. Pulling a "Stop the killing (in Vietnam)" sign from the bosom of her gown, she stepped calmly to the microphone and said to the president and his guests: "You go to church on Sunday and pray to Jesus Christ. If Jesus Christ was in this room tonight, you would not dare drop another bomb."[26]

As might be expected, the reaction of the president's guests was swift: Bob Hope decried the homily as "shameful"; Billy Graham was reported to have a "purple" cast to his face; Martha Mitchell suggested that the aspiring preacher be torn limb from limb. The dazed Conniff, being possessed of both tact and a sensitivity for the delicate protocol demanded under such conditions, restored the existential and symbolic weight of the shaken civil religion by ending the program with "God Bless America." That which God joins, it would seem, cannot be put asunder by woman either.

Thus far, I have used rather general terms about this "civil religion' of ours. Furthermore, I have been focusing upon secondary, often popularized, accounts of civil-religious activity. Such an approach has been taken intentionally, for it is my purpose here to suggest that popular norms and popular beliefs are the inexorable forces which regulate and propel our colloquies between God and country. Rhetorical failures in the civil-religious realm make news. They do so precisely because the agencies which regulate the interactions between church and state are fundamentally rooted in the American folkway. As we shall observe in Chapter 4, the popular constraints placed upon religio-political discourse earmark it as generically distinctive, as "communication of a sort." Were this not the case, Billy Bright, Billy Graham, Richard Nixon, Harry Truman, and Norman Vincent Peale would not know how to talk about America's religious heritage, and their communicative decisions would be made in the absence of rhetorically comforting standards. Too, were the ground rules which implicitly guide such discourse not known in a popular way, the miscues by Adlai Stevenson and Carol Feraci would have gone unheralded. Fossil rhetoric though it may be, its platitudinous regularity makes it important sociologically and renders it a vital object for scholarly inquiry.

American Civic Piety: Its Panorama

In 1970, Pat Boone, George Otis, and Harold Bredesen authored a passionate, chilling pamphlet entitled *The Solution to Crisis—America*. The book is interesting on a number of fronts. It is a rare contemporary warning of Communist subversion in the United States; it is consciously reactionary in its theology; and its zealous, prophetic cast is overshadowed only by its evangelistic concern for uniting spirituality and an improved political instinct in the American people. A short excerpt from the pamphlet reveals its tones more dramatically:

> This is God's blazing message to America in this hour—and *it is without question its very last chance.*
>
> This is the time to energize these spiritual weapons for the salvation of our land. It must be done *immediately, fervently, with faith, and with tears!*
>
> If this is done by the Christian people with all of their heart immediately, and with perseverance, this land shall not only be saved, but there shall also explode from this united prayer-power the most astounding revival in all history.
>
> MORE POWERFUL THAN
> TEN THOUSAND HYDROGEN BOMBS
>
> We have declared spiritual war on God's enemies and our enemies. NOW LET'S WAGE IT! [27]

Subsequent to writing the pamphlet, author Boone passed on a copy to the president of the United States—Richard Nixon. The contrast in emotional fervor between the pamphlet and Nixon's letter of appreciation[28] is a thing of rhetorical beauty to behold:

THE WHITE HOUSE
Washington

Dear Pat:

I want you to know how much I appreciate your thoughtfulness in letting me have a copy of your recording, "The Solution to Crisis— America," which you gave to Secretary Romney for me at the Religious Heritage Dinner on June 18. It was especially kind of you to remember me with this meaningful and timely message, and you may be sure I am pleased to have this evidence of faith and patriotism brought to my attention.

With my best wishes,

Sincerely,

Richard Nixon

Mr. Pat Boone
Beverly Hills, California 94710

The differences in the rhetorical styles of these two passages are significant. Where Boone & Co. excoriate, Nixon is blasé; the presidential circumspection contrasts sharply with the evangelism of the doomsayers; the traditional White House caution and optimism is nowhere to be seen in the pamphlet's gauntlet-dropping; most important, perhaps, is the obvious refusal by Nixon to match (or indirectly to give assent to) the confessional armor worn by the pamphlet's authors. The solution to America's crisis apparently did not reside in the presidential manor.

Official and Unofficial Civic Piety Contrasted
When one looks carefully at the tremendous array of God-and-country discourse in America, one is impressed by the great variation in *Weltanschauung*, in emotional drive, and in political partisanship imbedded therein. Boone and his co-authors provide evidence of what Robert Bellah would call an "heretical byway" of the civil religion, while Nixon's rhetoric travels timorously along the American mainstream. That public rhetoric is consistently chosen to body forth such nuances is significant. If we are to

believe Martin Marty, it is by inspecting such public expressions that we are able to differentiate among religious (here, religio-political) in-groups and out-groups:

> Americans tend to classify denominations in relation to their typical or mainstream status by a set of subtle contextual norms. *Most of them revolve around the dialogue of American churches with their environment.* The more exposed a group has been or becomes, the more its claims are eroded by its place in a pluralist society, the more it has been seen in harmony with main themes of national history, that much more does it belong. The more isolated, intransigent, withdrawn, the less exposed and eroded a group has been, no matter what its size and influence, the less it has come to be regarded as *a normative religious expression for America.* The largest remaining body of unexposed believers belong to what is known as sects and cults, and they can best be accounted for and located by this approach.[29] (Emphasis added.)

Taking Marty at his word, then, it should be possible to distinguish among those spokesmen who align themselves most closely with Bellah's "official" American civil religion (instances of which we have already seen and upon which we shall concentrate in Chapter 4), and those religious and political animals who stalk the American people from lairs far removed from 1600 Pennsylvania Avenue. Thus, the following chart indicates the breadth of church-state persuasion in America.

It should be evident from inspecting the chart that church-state rhetoric "factors" in varied and comp-lex ways in the United States. Not only do we speak extensively of things political and divine, but we do so within a bevy of what Bitzer has termed "rhetorical situations."[30] The range of speakers whose duty it is to fuel such rhetorical situations points up the myriad ways in which we rhetorically intertwine God and country. Characterizations of such rhetors might progress as follows:

1. Ecclesiastics: duly appointed or elected spokesmen for an organized body of religious believers.

2. Statesmen: duly appointed or elected governmental spokesmen.

3. Official civil religionists: ecclesiastics and statesmen who endorse the religious character of American society.

Rhetorical Activities in the Church-State Sector

Spokesmen	Rhetorical Foci		
	Church Issues	State Issues	Church-State Issues
Ecclesiastics	**1** Null case (E.g., conventional preaching on scriptural themes)	**2** E.g., Quaker commentary on warmongering	**3** E.g., Catholic lobbying on state aid to private schools
Statesmen	**4** E.g., governmental sanctions on inter-church disputes	**5** Null case (E.g., congressional debating, political campaigning, etc.)	**6** E.g., governmental regulation of Sabbath laws
Official Civil Religionists	**7** E.g., Thanksgiving proclamations by chief executive	**8** E.g., priestly invocation at political convention	**9** E.g., inaugural addresses
Unofficial Civil Religionists	**10** E.g., American Legion campaign for regular church attendance	**11** E.g., National Council of Christians and Jews remarking on political ethics	**12** E.g., Billy James Hargis speaking on Communist subversion
Irreligionists	**13** Null case (E.g. atheistic baiting of organized religion)	**14** Pure null case (Irreligionists, as a group, are apolitical)	**15** E.g., Madlyn Murray O'Hair on prayer in the public schools
Anti-secularists	**16** Null case (E.g., Doctrinal preaching on issues specific to the group of believers)	**17** Pure null case (Anti-secularists, as a group, are philosophically antipolitical)	**18** E.g., Jehovah Witnesses' refusal to engage in patriotic rituals

4. Unofficial civil religionists: spokesmen for political or religious (or quasi-religious) groups who promote interplay between civil and religious principles.
5. Irreligionists: Individuals or spokesmen for irreligious groups who attack organized religion and civil-religious ties.
6. Anti-secularists: Individuals or spokesmen for religious groups who, because of religious predilections, attempt to separate themselves from governmental imposition.

As indicated in the chart, church-state rhetoric in general concerns itself with religious, political, and religio-political matters. Moreover, the *dramatis personae* described above play their rhetorical parts in a variety of civil and religious contexts. The "null cases," those rhetorical activities which do not articulate in the main with civil-religious issues, are mentioned because collectively they comprise much of the discourse visited upon us daily; however, their direct relationship to church-state rhetoric is tangential in some cases and non-existent in others.

Having thus scouted out the general terrain of church-state rhetoric, we may now focus exclusively on discourse penetrated with "unofficial" civil-religious themes. It should be remembered, however, that in multi-faceted and significant ways, the rhetorical "fringe" activities exemplified in areas 2, 3, 4, 6, 15, and 18 of the chart affect the tenor and scope of the official and unofficial rhetoric of the American civil religion. The complete story of such complexities must be told another day, by another writer.[31]

The Rhetoric of Unofficial Civil Religion

In Chapters 2 through 4, I shall concentrate primarily on what has been termed here "official civil religious" rhetoric—the sort of talk engaged in by mainstream or establishment persons and groups. However, our national political faith is kindled and rekindled for many by a veritable potpourri of splinter groups or, as Martin Marty would have it, religio-political sects. The American Legion, the Catholic War Veterans, the Christian Economic Crusade, the D.A.R., the John Birch Society, the Church League of America, the American Coalition of Patriotic Societies, and innumerable other groups add color, intensity, drive, ambition, and grassroots appeal to our national religion. The fact that

Bellah chose to ignore such groups in his conceptualization of our national faith marks him as being inexcusably patrician in outlook. His rationale for dismissing such "sects" is, ostensibly, that the rhetoric of such groups does not embody the themes and attitudes so powerfully and historically captivating for the majority of the American people. While this may be so, the rhetoric of the civil-religious sects helps to place our "official" national religion in perspective, to vivify what is often so subtle in the rhetorical waters of the civil-religious mainstream.

The ontogeny of such sects is interesting. Apparently, the courtly, loose *gestalten* surrounding the official American civil religion does not provide for certain sub-groups in America the forthrightness and emotional fervor necessary for the realization of a religionized America. Thus, some civil-religious groups, like their purely religious counterparts, are spawned from "high church" religion. Marty describes the appeal of such sects as follows: "The thesis here is that negatively-oriented sects gain their current attractiveness from their attempt and relative success at isolating people from competing value systems; and that positively-oriented cults, usually gathered around charismatic persons or clans, succeed to the extent that they provide surrogates for interpersonal relations or attachment to significant persons in an apparently depersonalizing society."[32]

While the "underground" civil religions do not necessarily compete with their "official" counterparts, they sometimes manage to draw off enthusiasm from their parent bodies. At other times, the sects are embarrassingly vocal in their preachments, embarrassing, that is, as Pat Boone was for Richard Nixon. Thus, the "confessional relatives" of official civil religion are comprised of groups which embody sectarianism (both political and religious), activism, and overt ideology. While some such elements may, at times, wend their ways into the mainstream of our national faith, they do not universally distinguish the rhetoric surrounding it, as they do that of its second cousins.

Sectarianism

As mentioned previously, official civil religion characteristically seeks to effect a delicate balance between that which we render to God and to Caesar. Not so in the "heretical byways." For example, the Christian Government Movement (neé the Christian Amend-

ment Movement) is a longstanding pressure group whose eschaton is the Christianization of American political life. The group
lobbies vigorously, publishes frequently, and postures politically.
The basic principles of the group's constitution hint at just such
concerns:

> In the light of Scripture, the infallible Word of God, we hold these
> principles to be true:
> **1.** That all of life is to be lived in service to God; and that therefore a
> concern for national righteousness and justice is necessary for God's
> people.
> **2.** That men because of their willful rebellion against God do not
> know the way to political and national blessing.
> **3.** That the Lord Jesus Christ, having satisfied the demands of the Law
> and completed His work of redemption, is seated at the right hand of
> God the Father, and has been given all power and authority over the
> created universe, including governments.
> **4.** That Jesus Christ, through His Word and Spirit, reveals the
> principles of true justice for all of society and its institutions and
> directs Christians in their efforts to bring society into conformity with
> God's Word.
> **5.** That the church and the state are both institutions that have been
> called into being by God, and, although they are interrelated, neither
> should interfere with the proper functions of the other.
> **6.** That governments should make a public acknowledgment of the
> Kingship of Christ and respond obediently to His Word in their
> policies, programs, and decisions. Failure to do either of these is an
> affront to God and leads to judgment.
> **7.** That Christians are bound to make known to their leaders these
> principles, to make public confession for lack of obedience to
> these principles, and to seek true public justice and a proper
> acknowledgment of Christ's exalted position.[33]

When we compare such Christo-centered utterances to the
theologically bland fare usually served up at our national sacred
banquets, (e.g., "He who, in His mercy, watches over these United
States"), we begin to get a feeling for unofficial civil religion,
American style. Other groups, such as the National Association for
Christian Political Action, are even less expansive in outlook than
is the C.G.M. As we shall see in Chapter 4, the fundamentalist
perspective evidenced in the following passage (extracted from an
N.A.C.P.A. newsletter) is hardly characteristic of high-church civil
religion:

> . . . we are an evangelical, Bible-believing associaton of people
> who believe that Christ is Lord—Lord of all of life, wanting
> His servants everywhere working in obedience to Him. No work
> done for the Lord is in vain (I Cor. 15:58). All of life is therefore
> spiritual and sacred, or should be, for the Christian. There can never
> be two realms for the Christian, one spiritual, one secular,
> for no matter what he does, it must be done for the glory of
> God. That's why NACPA exists, to be the Body of Christ's arm at
> work in politics, trying to bring justice and peace through its
> various educational efforts (magazine, literature, research team of
> Christian political scientists, film, meeting with legislators, etc.).[34]

The sectarianism of unofficial civil religion also presents itself in avowedly political garb. For instance, the intensely political John Birch Society costumes itself in clerical robes during its "God and Country Rally" held annually in Belmont, Massachusetts. As Bellah insists, however: "For all the overt religiousity of the radical right today, their relation to the civil religious consensus is tenuous, as when the John Birch Society attacks the central American symbol of Democracy itself."[35] The John Bircher's motto replies sharply to Bellah: "less government, more responsibility, and with God's help, a better world."

Activism
Mention of the John Birch Society stimulates a second thought relative to unofficial civil religion: its viewpoint is distinctively partisan—such groups are more than willing to act out their political and religious convictions. While not all of the rhetoric of civil-religious sects is as strident as that of the Reverend Dallas F. Billington, its incorporation of hortatory themes is oftentimes just as unmistakable:

> "I want you . . . who are present to pray this prayer beside your
> bed every night: that God will kill [Madlyn Murray O'Hair]. . . .
> Now we have no right to go out and take a gun and kill her,
> but we can sure pray for God to kill her. I don't want you
> to stop there, I want you to pray to God to remove any judge
> or judges that keep us from having our Bible in our schools. . . .
> It is not wrong for you to pray God to destroy your enemy. . . .
> Is it wrong for us to pray to remove a judge that is to remove
> our Bibles? If we say for God to do it, have we committed any
> sin? No!"[36]

Perhaps the best known of the quasi-religious action groups is the Christian Anti-Communist Crusade, headed by that indomitable political cleric, Billy James Hargis. Hargis, more than most "one hundred percent Americans," has seized upon the unique, activating forces unleashed when God and country join together and arm themselves against leftist political thought:

> "I am asking one million Americans to collect a small stone from their rock garden (about the size of a silver dollar) wrap a Scripture provided on the back page of the *Weekly* around it, and mail it off to their impeachment-minded senators and congressmen," Hargis wrote.
>
> The Bible verse Hargis selected is appropriate to the occasion: "He that is without sin among you, let him first cast a stone. . . ."
>
> "That bunch of Pharisees in Jesus' time got the message, and so will these modern-day Pharisees who are willing to sacrifice the country so they can achieve their political dream."[37]

Richard Nixon did not face impeachment, it would appear, from any reluctance to act on the parts of some unofficial civil religionists.

Overt Ideology

Not all such "unofficial" groups are, of course, prone to such sectarian and activist impulses. Many patently political groups, however, do latch onto the "God stuff" which spurs so many to do so much. That is, many of the political groups occupying the starboard side of the American ship of state use theological concerns as a type of "rhetorical cover," as an all-encompassing, politically attractive tarpaulin with which to ward off the waves of liberal outrage which continually threaten to swamp them.

Perhaps the most obvious exemplar of the use of religion as a rhetorical front is the Church League of America, a domestic fact-gathering agency headquartered in Wheaton, Illinois. Among other things, the Church League's national office catalogues the names of "thousands of individuals" who, for example, write "an article or book attacking and ridiculing a major doctrine of the Christian Faith or the American way of life. . . ."[38] That such activities have an uncertain relationship with things theological appears to be of little concern to the "Church" League. Indeed, the entire matter of religion seems to hold little interest for them. In a three thousand-word pamphlet which purports to delineate the aims and programs of the organization, the word *church* is used eleven times (in each case, it refers to the name of the organization) and the word *God* is used but once (in the phrase "God is not dead").[39] Otherwise, the pamphlet busies itself with the political subversives who threaten to undermine America's traditional commitments.

Other instances of overt (some call it sham) religiosity abound in the rhetoric of the unofficial civil religionists. Literature issued by the National States Rights Party indicates that racism is the only bulwark with which to protect a "White Christian Civilization." Also, the Christian Anti-Communist Crusade, ostensibly aware that "communism" has become only a vaguely identifiable bogeyman for a generation of post-cold war Americans, has, of late, stepped up its religious appeals in what appears to be a desperate search for wellsprings of motivation with which to steel Americans against the indignities of socialistic thought. For example, from May through August of 1974, Christian Crusade leader Billy James Hargis, along with thirty young students (called the "All American Kids") from his American Christian College, trouped the country with a yankee-doodled, all-Christian, musical revue which encouraged audiences to take "a stand for Christ and conservatism."[40] The weaving and cross-weaving of God and country in Hargis's rhetoric serves the suasory function of creating what Berger and Pinard have called "a comprehensive universe of discourse,"[41] within which the indistinct goals of the deity become enveloped by, and then equated with, the more obvious ideals of the political group espousing them. It is because of such curious religious and political marriages, perhaps, that Sidney Mead has warned: "God, like Alice's Cheshire Cat, has sometimes threatened gradually to disappear altogether or, at most, to remain only as a disembodied and sentimental smile."[42]

To a lesser extent, the religio-political sword cuts both ways. That nationalism can become a rhetorical cover for certain kinds of religious persuasion was well demonstrated in one of the more curious documents to be published during the bicentennial celebrations. The World Home Bible League, an organization whose avowed political posture is normally (and necessarily) hard to distinguish, issued a paraphrased New Testament during the bicentennial—a book replete with a mawkishly patriotic cover and the title *Let Freedom Ring!* With the exception of the cover, a two-page "Americanish" introduction, and a dozen or so nondescript photos, the four-hundred-page volume contained nothing but the holy scriptures. Rhetorical expediency, it appears, was no stranger to our national celebrations.

Conclusion

While the burden of my investigation will be borne in the remainder of this essay by "mainstream" civil religion, I cannot dismiss or forget the continual, sometimes indelicate, interfaces shared by official and unofficial civil religion. Imagine the turmoil caused for the American Right when in December of 1973 the traditional Nativity scene was, via the agency of the American Civil Liberties Union, banned from occupying its accustomed place on the Ellipse near the White House. That such bifurcation could be effected between the central images of American government and American Christianity bestirred a good many citizens. "Are we to believe that the Constitution of the United States requires us to turn away the Baby Jesus from the White House?" angrily queried some. The A.C.L.U. countered by arguing, in effect, that the presence of the crèche constituted a "sectarian, activist, and overtly religious" incursion in matters primitively political. Although the day was won by the Civil Liberties Union (who, as is obvious, implicitly spoke on behalf of "official" civil religion in America), the commitment of those advocating "God, country, and conservatism" was only rekindled anew:

> And so the ancient story is repeated at the door of our national mansion. Once again, there is no room. Caesar may tax and count, posture and rule, without the annoying presence of Mary and Joseph, and the Babe lying in the manger. But let Caesar know that the Star in the East shines nevertheless. Let him know that, for all he might do, the true meaning of Christmas still swells great in the hearts of the American people. And let him be assured that he will yet have to deal with Christian soldiers.[43]

In this chapter, then, we have noted the intensity and power imbedded in the rhetoric of American civil piety. We have seen, too, that the civil-religious establishment in America is so pervasive as to qualify for the status of a rhetorical institution. In the following chapter, we shall attempt to understand how such institutionalization came about, focusing particularly on Robert Bellah's notion of an American civil religion and the extent to which this construct explains satisfactorily the phenomena we have been observing in this chapter, phenomena which, according to Gerald L. K. Smith, invariably serve to "het up" the American people.[44]

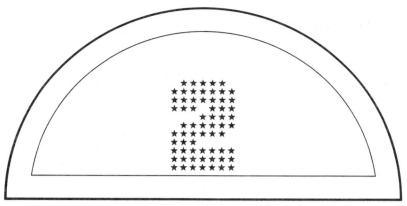

American Civic Piety: Traditional Explanations

"If the universe were material bound by inexorable law, still it needed a spiritual hypothesis. Even the Great Machine required a Divine Mechanic."[1] Thus did Sherwood Eddy account for the Founding Fathers' tendencies to spice their political statements with theological seasonings. Picking up on this theme, Robert Bellah has suggested that this "spiritual hypothesis" eventuated in a sort of national shadow religion, a religion used by the American people for making cosmic sense out of their collective strivings. As we have seen in Chapter 1, the lubricant used by the nation's "mechanics" (both Divine and otherwise) has been discourse of an unquestionably public variety.

Yet, whence derives this civic piety of ours? What are its roots? For what purpose was life first breathed into it? The answer to all three questions seems to be: civic piety in America is the rhetorical cognate of disestablishment; as such, its existence can be explained, in part, by noting the forces which led also to the "separation" of church and state.

In this chapter then, we shall examine the "traditional" interpretations which have been offered for the cordial rhetorical relations shared by government and religion in the United States. We shall look at philosophical, political, and other explanations which have been used to account for the amount and variety of church-state interaction found in America today. Subsequently, we shall examine with some scrutiny the "symbolic" interpretation offered by Robert Bellah and others, an interpretation which has

29

received widespread acclaim from scholars and laypersons alike. As we move through such rival explanations for the separation-coordination of organized religion and American government, we will be reminded once again that we are examining in disestablishment a phenomenon of manifest importance, a facet of our national character which has been termed "a greater revolutionary event than the mere political separation from Great Britain."[2]

The Roots of Disestablishment and Civic Piety

Although most informed scholars agree that the guarantee of religious freedom in the United States is one of its most fundamental and distinctive features as a nation, there are a wealth of competing explanations for why—given the socio-political environment of the eighteenth century—the American people, unlike their forebears in almost any other portion of the world, especially Europe, managed to escape internecine struggles between church and state. That the American people were uniquely able to escape such turmoil in their very beginnings, and yet to be regarded widely as citizens of a "religious nation," could be viewed merely as an interesting historical accident, did it not have such profound socio-political implications. Explanations for this symbiosis of religious and political institutions in the United States are rife. To some of these, we shall now turn.

Political Hypothesis
One of the most attractive explanations for church-state cordiality in America is that which treats disestablishment as a cultural integrator of society, a kind of "social inhibitor" which kept the rival theological factions which founded America from lunging at each others' jugular veins. Leo Pfeffer, a preeminent student of religious freedom in America, suggests that our earliest settlers were convinced "that the best way to keep from these shores the religious bloodshed, persecution, and intolerance that had plagued the old world was to maintain . . . a wall between church and state in the new world."[3] Other writers, however, are quick to point out that the mortice joints in such walls do not always hold. As Dennis Brogan comments, "Religion has been a notorious

dividing force where it was not identified with the state. Hence the Inquisition, the Penal Laws in Ireland, the waves of persecution and counter-persecution in France."[4] According to our "political" hypothesis, then, the colonists fashioned a rigorously secular government and provided it with a religious patina for largely sentimental reasons.

Many authorities would not credit the earliest Americans with such prescience, however. Some suggest that the settlers would have been just as apt to fall into the ageless religio-political nettles had it not been for the very facts of national survival themselves. For example, of the original thirteen colonies, only two, Virginia and Rhode Island, guaranteed full religious freedom to its people. Delaware and Maryland demanded Christianity. Pennsylvania, Delaware, North and South Carolina required assent to the divine inspiration of the Bible. Most of the remaining colonies demanded adherence to some sort of religious establishment.[5] As Bates notes, the eventuating religious toleration in America "was never isolated, as the myth would have it, from an economic or political background."[6] According to the political hypothesis, then, the colonists used civil-religious rhetoric as a surrogate for a church-state. Whatever else they were, our Founding Fathers were delightful pragmatists.

Philosophical Hypothesis
While admitting to the verity of the political hypothesis, other commentators account for the rhetorical copulation of church and state in America via alternative routes. For example, Higginbotham summarizes the position of many intellectual historians (like Perry Miller) when he argues that the American "experiment" in church-state polity was but an extension (a radical one, but an extension nonetheless) of certain philosophical currents that were sweeping across Europe and elsewhere in the late seventeenth and eighteenth centuries. Says Higginbotham: "The Revolution needed religious foundations to match the political underpinnings provided by Locke and Jefferson. If the Enlightenment led educated men to rationalism or deism, traditional Christianity still loomed large in the lives of the great majority of Americans, most of whom were Protestants of the left wing or Calvinist variety."[7]

Thus, not only was such disestablishment necessary for economical-political reasons, but it also provided a kind of philosophical frame for the burgeoning governmental structures—a socially acceptable, ultimately political rationale for seeking independence. The effects of such a "grand scheme" on colonization were pronounced: "Each citizen bore responsibility, moral no less than political" argues Edwin Gaustad.[8] That the revolutionary era managed to weld the potentially competing philosophical systems of government and religion was no small feat. That it could fashion out of them a viable, pragmatic spirit of independence—of America from her mother country and of church from state—was as unexpected as it was important.

Serendipitous Hypothesis
When accounting for such a broad and complex movement as the American "experiment" in church-state relations, the simplest hypothesis is often the most attractive. A growing number of scholars are beginning to demythologize our national infancy by suggesting that a host of confusing, often competing forces rather accidentally conspired to establish American civic piety as a going institution. That is, while some would have us believe that the fervor with which disestablishment was sought was surpassed solely by Jonathan Edwards's own holy trek into the American wilderness, others remind us that the American colonists were as a whole "not very much interested in religion, a fact which, if it did not favor the health of churches, nevertheless did indicate a spirit which could accept Jefferson's interpretation of the meaning of the First Amendment."[9]

Still, while some of the colonists may have been nonplussed by religion, their millenarian brethren viewed young America as constituting a New Israel, a land replete with an overwhelming sense of religious destiny. In the light of such contrasting views of the importance of religion, then, the American civil religion may well have been erected on the pedestal of happenstance, no clearcut theological mandate for a super-religious government being apparent.

Perhaps most skillfully articulated by Bernard Bailyn, the serendipitous hypothesis thus encourages us to view the disestablishment of religion (and, subsequently, the institutionalizing of American civic piety) as emanating from a veritable labyrinth of forces—social, philosophical, religious, economic, historical, political, and accidental:

The disestablishment of religion was neither an original goal nor completely a product of the Revolution. Its roots lay deep in the colonial past, in circumstances that Jonathan Parsons described as a "random way of settling ministers and churches, together with a vile contempt of creeds and confessions . . . all seem to jumble together, and make mere *hodgepodge.*" These unplanned, unexpected conditions, lacking in completeness and justification, were touched by the magic of Revolutionary thought, and were transformed."[10]

This is a "climate of the times" hypothesis, a position which holds that America was founded by a good number of church-goers who, perhaps quite inadvertently, managed to enwrap all of their burgeoning social and political systems with the mantle of religious language. Equally, they were political tinkerers despite themselves, persons willing to experiment with unprecedented social compacts. The collage of forces which acted upon them was apparently sufficient, in any event, to replace European models of church-state relations with a national attitude of all things in their proper places . . . including God.

For a number of reasons, then, disestablishment came to America. When it came, however, a void was created, a void which eventually came to be filled by American civic piety (among other things). But for civic piety to "work," it too had to have special attractiveness for the nation's citizens. It had to "do" something for the American people which they chose not to have done by legal or constitutional means.

Symbolic Hypothesis

Not surprisingly, the man who popularized the phrase, "American civil religion," has his own peculiar explanation for its existence. In attempting to account for the emergence of our national faith, Robert Bellah burrows for his rationale deep within the human condition when he argues that a society must make its ideals sacred through appropriate symbolism and develop its own metaphysic if it is to function with maximum emotional efficiency. Our national ethos, according to Bellah, is one which needs to explain itself to itself in grand and idealistic fashion.

Bellah's explanation thus constitutes the symbolic hypothesis for understanding American civic piety. According to such a perspective, our nation has had a special (not necessarily unique) need to create a galaxy of symbols with which to articulate its collective goals as a people, its most fundamental and demanding values, its heritage and its destiny. Ostensibly, the red, white, and blue bunting, the presidential seals, the deistic imprimaturs on our coins, the Christmas messages, the Fourth of July oratory, the Lincolns, the Eisenhowers, the Nixons, and God in His heaven, collectively participate in a symbolic cacophony from which Americans derive their national self-understanding. According to such a viewpoint, then, the symbolic abyss created by disestablishment was filled by an American civil religion.

In his research in the area, Bellah focused almost exclusively on what I have termed (in Chapter 1) "official" civil religion. Indeed, Bellah concentrated most of his analysis on the "high priest" of our national faith, the president of the United States. From such an exalted perspective, Bellah's American civil religion constitutes an attractive explanation for the widespread existence of civic piety. Like any group of religious believers, Americans needed their prophets (e.g., Benjamin Franklin), their patriarchs (Washington), their martyrs and their redeemers (Lincoln). Generally, Americans expect their chief executives to perform the role of shaman (because presidents devote only part of their working time to religious tasks),[11] while roving, but full-time, civil religionists like Billy Graham are viewed as the workaday "diviners," priests who read the will of the gods in omens:

> America's soul: patriotism, morality, respect for law, faith, social justice, brotherhood among people of diverse backgrounds. This is the very soul of America but we are in danger of losing our soul, and the boys in the military may soon ask if it is worth dying for. Unless our soul is restored, the best men in America will begin to ask if it is worth going into politics for. *Unless our soul is renewed and restored.* Jesus asked the question long ago: What shall it profit a man or a nation if they gain the whole world and lose the soul.[12]

In addition to its distinct personalities, the American civil religion has its holy places (the White House), its amulets (Nixon's lapel flags), its saints (Norman Vincent Peale) and its sinners (the Berrigans), its baptisms (the first grader's pledge of allegiance) and its confirmations (often administered by military chaplains). Although it is highly non-denominational, our national faith is nevertheless creedal (i.e., nationalistic). Our grade schools "provide the place of instruction . . . in the sacred history of the civil religion."[13] This "sacred canopy" of symbols, according to Peter

Berger, performs basic and important functions for a society: "The 'gains' of theodicy for a society are to be understood in a way analogous to those for the individual. Entire collectivities are thus permitted to integrate anomic events, acute or chronic, into the *nomos* established in their society."[14]

The popularity of Bellah's symbolic hypothesis is remarkable. As Thomas and Flippen indicate,[15] almost all of the major texts in the sociology of religion have accepted Bellah's thesis, star-spangled tabernacle and all. Bellah himself has remarked somewhat immodestly, "the phrase 'civil religion in America' . . . took on a life of its own . . . has been picked up by the *New York Times* and by the popular newsweeklies, . . . has inspired books, essays, and symposia."[16] Nevertheless, some criticism of Bellah's notion of an American civil religion can be offered, the most fundamental of which centers around the theoretical power it is able to muster in explaining the existence of civic piety in America.

The "American Civil Religion" as Theoretical Construct

Perhaps the most potentially devastating critique to be made of Bellah's hypothesis is offered by John Wilson, who asserts that civic piety has been incorrectly labeled a civil religion by Bellah. Employing a purist's understanding of the construct *religion,* Wilson argues that the refrains Bellah found imbedded in presidential discourse do not "manifest the kind of interrelatedness, institutionalization, and coherence of expression which would warrant identifying them as positive evidence for a developed and differentiated religion" in the strictest sense of that word.[17] Wilson is even more specific in his charges when he defines "real religion" as providing for:

(1) cultic aspects to the phenomena, i.e., provision for periodic (frequent) ceremony or ritual which provides definitive interpretation of it; (2) recognized leadership offices invested with effective authority; (3) explicity defined means of participation in the religion (thus establishing the grounds of membership); (4) at least implicit delineation of beliefs—if not "correct belief"; (5) influence upon behavior at one or more levels and in a manifest way; (6) finally, and perhaps most important, a coherence of the above in order for the conception of religion to be applicable. Beliefs and behavior must have some manifest relationship to each other.[18]

According to such criteria, Bellah's American civil religion does not pass the muster.

An American Civil Religion?

The implicit response that Bellah makes, of course, is that he was arguing analogically (as I have done when offering the metaphorical extensions of Bellah's conception included above). That the bulk of his argument stands on the stilt-like legs of metaphor seems not to bother Bellah:

> In a sense, and not in a trivial sense, civil religion in America existed from the moment the winter 1967 issue of *Daedalus* was printed. . . . By saying [this] I do not mean that the notion was arbitrary, fanciful, or a myth, in the perjorative sense of that word. But I do mean that it was what Alfred Schutz would have called a social construction of reality . . . [as Schutz says] "We live in the description of a place and not in the place itself."[19]

Thus, Bellah is arguing that his metaphorical interpretation has heuristic value and that the concept of "religion" provides him with explanatory power not made available via alternative conceptualizations of the same phenomena. Lest the reader become impatient with what may seem to be semantic nit-picking, it should be noted that were we not to allow Bellah the argumentative expansiveness of his "religion" metaphor, many of his interpretations of civil-religious discourse would fall asunder, as we shall see later in this essay.

Some resolution to the debate appears to derive from our assuming a Durkheimian-functionalist approach to the question. That is, by looking at the distinctive jobs traditional religion is said to perform for the individual believer, and by judging Bellah's "religion" in the light of such criteria, we may arrive at a clearer understanding of the controversy. Listed below, then, are what Thomas O'Dea sees as the most common tasks accomplished by traditional religious organizations:

1. Supportiveness—some supra-human being provides consolation to the oppressed, the frustrated, and the deprived.

2. Priestly ministration—explicit religious doctrine and guidance are provided for the religious community.

3. Normative base—standards of judgment for determining the rightness or wrongness of conduct are provided.

4. Prophetic statements—an ethical ideal is held up by which the believer may guide his future actions.
5. Identity—the believer is defined as part of a larger community of believers who have an ultimate meaning for life.
6. Growth—the individual is helped to grow intellectually and psychologically within the framework of the religion.
7. Expressivity—important, psychologically satisfying means of expression are provided for in religious worship.
8. Renewal—through ritual, deep-seated values are refreshed and given new meaning for the believer.
9. Hope—religions oftentimes hold out the possibility that there will be a magical intervention in human affairs.
10. Predictability—patterned explanations of life are given, often by scriptural pronouncements.
11. Authority—some over-arching standard is offered which encourages or castigates alternative courses of actions.[20]

When applying such standards to Bellah's American civil religion, we must keep in mind the corpus from which he derived much of his conceptualization—the inaugural addresses of the presidents of the United States, a seemingly small body of data from which to posit the existence of anything as grand as a national faith. Still, in a severely limited sense, the American civil religion occasionally performs some of the functions of traditional religion. In Lincoln's second inaugural, for example, we find elements of supportiveness, of a normative base, and of prophetic impetus for a war-ravaged people. Too, Kennedy's maiden presidential speech attempts in oblique fashion to provide identity, predictability, and renewal for the new frontiersmen he was addressing. Most of the other presidential inaugurals contain possibilities for expressivity and, on occasion, authoritative bases upon which the American people may found courses of action they are contemplating.

However, to look for aspects of doctrine, of psychological growth, or of "magical intervention" by an immanent God in presidential inaugurals would be to break the back of the fragile metaphorical edifice Bellah attempted to erect in 1967. Indeed, if we apply O'Dea's criteria of interrelatedness and coherence of expression to the apparent religiosity of presidential inaugurals, then even Lincoln and Kennedy would have to be viewed as playing at the religious game. As Alley correctly asserts, if there is a civil

religion, "the strength of presidential personalities [tends] to construct a new civil religion in every generation."[21] In the light of
such "religion-like" remarks of the American presidents, then, to
find a civil *religion* in America would be to distort the concept of
religion unnecessarily. At the very least, Bellah has found a
"religion" that, say, a staunch Roman Catholic, or an orthodox
Jew, or an Episcopalian would hardly see as rivaling their respective faiths. At best, the American civil religion is a political version
of Unitarianism.

That pioneer Bellah has found "true" religion in the inaugural
wilderness becomes even less certain when we look at the
chronology of civil religion in America. As O'Dea states, all "real"
religions experience certain dilemmas when, as is their natural
course, they undergo institutionalization (i.e., when their doc-
trines and modes of worship become modified and regularized
within a definable organizational framework.) That is, as a religion
matures, there develop mixed motivational states within its
members, routinization of ritual, internal bureaucratic rivalries,
"legalization" of ethical beliefs, and sharp differences of opinion
between the religion and the prevailing political order which permits its existence.[22] Most modern religions, it seems clear, have
faced each of these problems in one form or another as they have
moved toward institutionalization.

The American civil religion, on the other hand, appears to
have undergone no such sociological adolescence. As we have
seen, the motives of its citizen-believers were thoroughly mottled
as far back as the 1700s. Furthermore, although ritual has always
characterized civic piety, it is hardly routinized in the way that
most "real" religious rituals come to be. Because the organizational structure of the American civil religion has always been
amorphously defined (e.g., any mainstream minister, priest, or
rabbi will "do" for the necessary invocation), the bureaucracy,
whatever little bit of it there is, has always functioned rather
smoothly. Also, according to any standard definition of doctrine,
no such phenomenon has ever been a significant part of a national
faith articulated by both a Kennedy and a Nixon in the same
decade. Most important, of course, is the fact that there has never
been anything but the most cordial relationship between the
American civil religion and the United States government itself, a
fact stemming in large part from the almost total identification

both entities share as civic pietists. Thus, by reverse reasoning, it appears that because it never has experienced the problems most formal religions have undergone, the American civil religion—as an analogue to institutionalized religion—is not made of the philosophical and sociological stuff of which "religions" have been traditionally constituted.[23]

In disallowing Bellah his use of the term *religion*, I am in no way suggesting that his research has been for nought. Indeed, Bellah has brought to his subject a penetrating sort of insight. Equally, my point here is not to quibble with terminology. Rather, I am suggesting that by employing the construct of religion, Bellah committed himself to all of its attendant dimensions and implications. Had he used Wilson's happier conceptualization of "civic piety," Bellah might have avoided a number of theoretical waterloos.

This is not to say, of course, that Bellah is wrong and Wilson right. After all, Wilson can be charged with theoretic provincialism (possibly even anachronism) when he insists on reserving the term *religious* for those activities which take place in churches. Moreover, there is some smattering of scholasticism to be found in Wilson's arguments, especially when he insists on debating the existence of a "thing" called civil religion. Ultimately, of course, the Wilson-Bellah debate will be settled on the most pragmatic of grounds: the extent to which their respective models are capable of generating theoretically elegant understandings of the phenomena they have chosen to observe. While the data are not yet in on Wilson, the forthrightness with which Bellah has presented his conceptualization permits us a brief examination of its theoretical worthiness.

The American Civil Religion as a Reified Construct

As mentioned previously, most of the commentary made of Bellah's stimulating essay has focused on the positive and negative valences the national religion appears to possess. However, few writers have questioned Bellah's theoretical starting point—that the religious refrains in presidential speeches can best be understood as manifestations of a civil religion in America. It would seem, however, that if Bellah's initial assumption is faulty (or insufficiently developed), then any subsequent extrapolations made of such an assumption are either logically premature or founded on benign premises. As Wilson states, Bellah has not "made a compelling case that the relevant phenomena [he identified] . . . become intelligible only in these terms."[24]

To obtain a clearer perspective of the issue, let us review Bellah's own seminal statement on the matter of civil religion: "This article argues not only that there is such a thing [as a civil religion], but also that this religion—or *perhaps better, this religious dimension*—has its own seriousness and integrity and requires the same care in understanding that any other religion does."[25] (Emphasis added.) In talking about "this religious dimension," Bellah's errors are more than syntactical. What he meant to add, of course, is "this religious dimension *of rhetoric.*" That is, Bellah discovered not "religion," but interesting rhetorical assertions. His civil religion was his own hypostatization, and Bellah, in expanding upon his "religious" hypothesis rather than upon his rhetorical discovery, opened himself up to all of the very real dangers that reification creates for analysts of the human condition. At the risk of sounding presumptuous, it appears that Bellah was somewhat taken in by the civic piety he set out to explain. In creating his religion out of the humble stuff of which rhetoric is made, Bellah, not unlike Doctor Frankenstein himself, became the first meal of this rhetoric turned religion turned reified monster.

To explain Bellah's construction of a national religion, one need look no further than Bellah's primary corpus of data—presidential inaugurals—which contain the most rhetorically astute, emotionally compelling, and historically sanctioned civil-religious discourse American politicians have managed to fashion in two centuries. At the hands of rhetorical giants like Jefferson, Lincoln, Roosevelt, and Kennedy, even an eminent twentieth-century sociologist could hardly avoid casting his analyses in sacral tones and heralding the existence of an American civil religion. That Bellah perhaps overreacted to the discourse he inspected is understandable when one recognizes that passages like the following are likely to cause even the most hard-headed sociologist to swoon: "This is the hope that beckons us onward in this century of trial. This is the work that awaits us all, to be done with bravery, with charity, and with prayer to Almighty God."[26]

Bellah's fatal flaw of responding to his own reifications may be accounted for by his tendency to adopt a patrician perspective of the American civil religion. From the exalted position of presidential ceremonies, all appears to be right, good, true, . . . and sacred. The churlish expendiency of the Church League of America seems far removed from such rarified pinacles. Viewing the American civil religion through the multi-colored lenses of brand-spanking new presidents, however, is not unlike building sociological theory of young America by exclusively interviewing the acneless kids on Pepsi commercials.

At crucial points, it would seem, Bellah has unfortunately sacrificed his prodigious analytical detachment to speak solemnly and idealistically of the religion he found and, later, loved too well. Indeed, Bellah's own rhetoric contains many of the same reverent, hopeful tones with which presidents attempt to invigorate their maiden speeches. For example, when commenting on the American Indians, Bellah had this to say about civil religion:

> They point out to us that though we are the bearers of a tradition that has its own integrity, it is not a self-sufficient tradition. The survival of all of us on earth today, a survival that, as Norman O. Brown has pointed out, is itself only a utopian hope, depends upon our pooling of all man's cultural resources. If America can have any meaning and value in the future it is only a relative value, only as part of a greater encompassing whole.[27]

Of such stuff, any inaugural speaker would be proud.

Recently, Charles Henderson (himself a fascinating scholar of civil religion) has hinted at the reason for what I am here describing as Bellah's theoretical miscues.[28] Reviewing Bellah's book, *The Broken Covenant*, Henderson wrote:

> But Robert Bellah is not only writing *about* religion in America, he is also a spokesman *for* religion. He is personally involved in and committed to a particular faith which he has worked out over the last quarter century. . . . In *The Broken Covenant* Bellah writes with precisely that double vision. He speaks as a sociologist who steps back to take the long view, the analytical view; and he speaks as an advocate of the most vital elements of the religion he describes. His book records not only those thoughts and perceptions which come to him as a result of logical analysis; he speaks also from the heart.[29]

The point I am attempting to enforce in this chapter is that Bellah's "double vision" does some amount of sociological and theoretical damage, no matter what theological benefits may inhere in his several analyses.

Conclusion

Several conclusions seem warranted by this brief analysis of Bellah's American civil religion. The first is that I have been talking here about *Bellah's* American civil religion, a social construction of reality invented by Robert Bellah for the purpose of explaining certain human events. As Martin Marty notes, the American civil religion exists much as the Middle Ages exist for the scholar—both are convenient labeling devices by which human activities can be described or explained efficiently.[30] In labeling phenomena thusly, Bellah served an important function—he dramatically pointed out certain events and ideas which had hitherto been ignored completely, treated as trivial, or explained insufficiently. But because Bellah manufactured a construct, and subsequently treated the construct as if it existed in fact, he failed to investigate alternative explanations for his data base. There are other methods for interpreting the religious refrains we find in presidential discourse, methods which appear to be aligned closely with the observed realities themselves.

In the following pages, I shall offer just such an alternative method, taking my lead from historian John Wilson. In a provocative essay entitled "A Historian's Approach to Civil Religion," Wilson politely refuses to accept the notion of an American civil religion, concluding his essay with the observation: "In a historical perspective I think it is difficult to arrive at the judgment that there is in American society an institutionalized, well-developed, and differentiated civil religion, a tradition parallel to and interrelated with other religious traditions in our culture."[31] Alternatively, Wilson muses, other models may prove to be more flight worthy than the religious paradigm constructed by Bellah.[32] As to what such models may be, however, Wilson is uncomfortably vague. In Chapter 3, I shall offer a relatively explicit alternative to Bellah's model. Thereafter, I shall attempt to apply this alternative understanding to the very sorts of phenomena Bellah himself studied and to determine if a rhetorical model of civic piety thereby sheds new light on a topic which has become unnecessarily beclouded. Before turning to such matters, one should be reminded that no other approach could have been envisioned had not Bellah imaginatively and pointedly isolated such phenomena for analysis in the first place. As Alley has commented, "Allowing his assumption, [Bellah] produces an impressive case."[33]

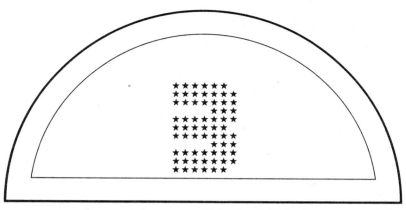

American Civic Piety:
An Alternative Understanding

THIS CONTRACT, made ___Each___ day of __Each Month__ between ___the United States Goverment___, herein called the "first party", and __Organized Religion__, herein called the second party";

WITNESSETH: That for and in recognition and performance of the covenants contained herein on the part of both parties in the manner hereinafter specified, let both parties recognize that: A) Religion is capable of providing an ultimate meaning system for its adherents; B) Government is able to exert coercive power on the affairs of its citizens; and C) Both government and religion wield considerable rhetorical power both within their respective sectors and across sectors.

This contract is made by the aforementioned parties and is accepted upon the following conditions, and it is agreed that each of the terms hereinafter specified shall be a condition. The breach, default, failure or violation of any one or more thereof shall entitle the innocent party to terminate this contract. In addition, should any first party official fail to abide by the stated conditions or in any other manner fail to pay tacit homage to religion, he or she shall be branded un-American and declared non-electable; and, should any member of any second party body fail to abide by the stated conditions or in any other manner to deny God's approbation of governmental policy, both foreign and domestic, he or she shall be labeled radical and denied an opportunity to offer the benediction at political gatherings.

Let it furthermore be agreed to that:

1. The guise of complete separation between the first party and the second party will be maintained by both parties.

2. The guise of existential equality between the first party and the second party will be maintained by both parties, but the second party's realm shall be solely that of the rhetorical.

3. First party rhetoric will refrain from being overly religious and second party rhetoric will refrain from being overly political.

4. Neither of the aforementioned parties shall, in any fashion whatsoever, make known to the general populace the exact terms of the contract contained herein.

— This agreement shall inure to the benefit of both parties, and their successors in interest.

WITNESS our hands, the day and year first above written.

The Government Incarnate
_____
FIRST PARTY

Mainstream Religion
_____
SECOND PARTY

The American Citizenry-as-Audience
_____
WITNESS

_____

It does not take a legal scribe to determine that the above document possesses more metaphorical than adjudicative value. Yet, as we shall see in this chapter, the document is, nonetheless, quite "real." That is, I shall be arguing here that (1) the contracting "parties" were knowing, if not conscious, signatories; (2) the apparently flacid "terms" of the contract are really quite binding on those who subscribe to its contents; and (3) the "contract" has been renegotiated with unflagging regularity throughout the political experience of this nation. It is hoped that this *rhetorical* interpretation of church-state relations in America will provide an attractive, alternative explanation for the genesis and perpetuation of American civic piety. In Chapter 4, we shall see that the functions, themes, and characteristics of civil-religious discourse can best be understood by viewing such rhetoric via this contractual image.

An Overview of the "Contract"

Should the wary reader contrast my critique of Bellah's "religion" (in Chapter 2) and the "contract" with which we began this chapter, he or she might be tempted to cry "foul!" After all, I too shall be using metaphor when attempting to account for the religion-filled political rhetoric prevalent in the United States. However, my questioning of Bellah's conceptualization was not meant to disparage metaphorical argument but simply to warn against an overextension of it. Thus, I shall try to use metaphor consciously, fully aware of the conceptual pitfalls which accompany such an approach. Moreover, I shall not treat this contractual image as constituting probative argument, but simply as one device scholars may use to illuminate complex phenomena. Also, I shall attempt to select a metaphorical map—a legal contract—which appears to explain faithfully the fact-territory being dealt with here—public rhetoric—without compromising the argument with intentional fallacies.

The choice of the legal-contractual metaphor was not a capricious one. For as one looks at the amount and intensity of civil-religious discourse in America, one may be impressed by what seems to be the unerring rhetorical choreography exhibited by religious and governmental spokesmen alike. The timing, phrasing, and elegance of our national prayers appear to emanate from persons who know full well their roles in the rhetorical chorus line. Civic piety, in America at least, emerges not so much from blind, momentary passion, but from a knowing, practiced, thoroughly pragmatic understanding of the suasory arabesques demanded when God and country kick up their heels rhetorically.

The Contractual Metaphor

Haltingly, to be sure, Peter Berger has suggested that "our political life continues to be infused with religious symbols, religious

rhetoric, and religious functionaries" all of which appear to constitute "a *de facto* political establishment of religion. . . ."[1] Gustav
Weigel makes the point more directly: "Secular society today is
trying to *make a deal* with the churches. It is saying: Give us your
unswerving support in the pursuit of the objectives we have
before us; in return we will cover you with honor."[2] (Emphasis
added.) Surely, such talk of *de facto* "deals" being made between
God and Caesar extracts much of the poetry from civic piety. This
is precisely my point—that the government of the United States
and America's organized religious bodies have entered into a very
practical compact rooted in an understanding of the role public
rhetoric plays in the minds of its citizens and of the stabilizing
effect public messages can have on their lives.

In opting for this contractual metaphor, I am obviously taking
a goodly number of historical liberties. To account for two hundred years of rhetoric and rhetors with so humble a vehicle as the
contract beginning this chapter is to be reductionistic with a
vengeance. The church-state story in the United States is hardly a
simple one, as we have seen in the early portions of Chapter 2.
Mountains of conflicting motivations, thousands of diverse personalities, and scores of historical, political, theological, and
sociological currents have conspired to fashion the rhetorical
relationships which contemporary Americans now observe being
shared by government and religion. Thereby denied truly
probative value, our contractual metaphor's usefulness lies in the
murky waters of the heuristic.

Yet it can teach us well. Consider, for example, the day upon
which the terms of this contract were first made publicly manifest.
It was a day during which the constant wrangling of the delegates
to the Constitutional Convention threatened to destroy the
delicate cordiality so recently and precariously effected among the
political spokesmen for the American people. Local interests and
personal ambitions promised to bring down the new edifice of
nationhood constructed during the war with Great Britain. In-
fighting, political intrigue, and plain home-grown American con-
trariness loomed ominously in 1787. In the midst of this pre-
Constitutional rancor, an elderly gentleman slowly rose from his
chair at a crucial moment. It was "Benjamin Franklin, the elder
statesman"[3] who made the following address:

Mr. President: The small progress we have made after four or five weeks close attendance and continual reasonings with each other—our different sentiments on almost every question, several of the last producing as many noes as ayes, is methinks a melancholy proof of the imperfection of the human understanding. . . .

I have lived, Sir, a long time, and the longer I live, the more convincing proofs I see of this truth—that God governs in the affairs of men. And if a sparrow cannot fall to the ground without His Notice, is it probable that an empire can rise without His aid? . . .

I, therefore, beg leave to move that, henceforth, prayers imploring the assistance of Heaven, and its blessings on our deliberations, be held in this assembly every morning we proceed to business, and that one or more of the clergy in this city be requested to officiate in that service.[4]

Benjamin Weiss, apologist for the American civil religion, remarks that following Franklin's address, "the members of the Convention soon demonstrated a different attitude of willingness to give and take and the *Constitution* began to take form."[5] Apocryphal though the specifics of the tale may be, and egregiously specious though Weiss's casual argument may appear, it seems clear that Franklin's address may well be viewed as an important symbolic benchmark in the history of civil-religious discourse in America. Franklin's "speech" evidences many of the traits we associate with contemporary religio-political rhetoric: (1) it achieves its fullest expression during moments of crisis; (2) it taps a dimension—religion—that is rhetorically compelling for many Americans; (3) it reduces inordinately complex issues to their most basic, patently religious, understructures; (4) it reaffirms the coordinated, but separate, roles men and God play in the affairs of this nation; and (5) its grand abstractness creates a totemic structure around which all Americans may happily rally. No matter what cynical historians may say about Franklin's speech being a sagacious, diversionary tactic (a harbinger of labor-management's "cooling off period"?), God has settled many a rhetorical crisis in the history of the American people.

While some may still cling tenaciously to the view that Franklin's speech was (in the language of the American civil religion) a "genuine outpouring of deep religious commitment," it would be unwise to dismiss casually the significant politico-rhetorical dimensions of his act, or to deny the verity of Peter Berger's interpretation of such "sacred canopies":

> If one imagines oneself as a fully aware founder of a society, a kind of combination of Moses and Machiavelli, one could ask oneself the following question: How can the future continuation of the institutional order, now established *ex nihilo*, be best ensured? [The answer seems to be to] let the people forget that this order was established by men and continues to be dependent upon the consent of men. Let them believe that, in acting out the institutional programs that have been imposed upon them, they are but realizing the deepest aspirations of their own being and putting themselves in harmony with the fundamental order of the universe. In sum: Set up religious legitimations. There are, of course, wide historical variations in the manner in which this has been done. In one way or another, the basic recipe was followed throughout most of human history. And, actually, the example of Moses-Machiavelli figuring the whole thing out with cool deliberation may not be as fanciful as all that. There have been very cool minds indeed in the history of religion.[6]

The coolest of such minds in our colonial history may well have been that of the gentleman from Philadelphia.

Rhetorical Nature of the Contract

If the latter part of this chapter, I shall speak more directly of the specific terms agreed to by the spokesmen of God and government. Before doing so, however, it may profit us to examine two of the more general features of the agreement: its rhetoricalness and its flexibility.

If my contractual metaphor has any value, it is that of pointing out the extent to which the American people have relied on public rhetoric to extricate themselves from uncomfortable political and social binds. Perhaps because rhetoric is such a useful and malleable entity, the American populace have long agreed to the maxim: that which we cannot accomplish *de jure,* we shall effect *per rhetorica.* Thus, if America could not survive amicably as a totally secular state, it had to be provided with a religious mantle through the agency of public discourse. If organized religion demands a say-so in the political and ethical life of the nation, it must be given precisely that—a *say-so.* And if the rhetorics of government and religion clash, resolution or sublimation must be effected through more rhetoric.

That public discourse has been chosen to effect and to maintain the delicate relationships shared by church and state is no happenstance. The very nature of rhetoric itself earmarks it as a perfect candidate for such a herculean task: (1) while the effects which rhetoric produces are sometimes painfully tangible, rhetoric itself is thoroughly ethereal; (2) rhetorical engagements are transitory events, a kind of symbolic quicksilver; (3) rhetorical power can be placed in the hands of many persons (especially in a large, heterogenous society) without existential conflict necessarily ensuing; (4) given the correct emotional and attitudinal circumstances, rhetoric is an incredibly potent force which can advance and retard a culture's ideologies. Because it is possessed of such qualities, rhetoric is a most appropriate agency for propelling a society's facts as well as its fictions.

While irreligionists like Madlyn Murray O'Hair may well decry the inroads which religion has made into political life in America,[7] our history clearly argues that rhetorical contracts, not legal ones, have been American religion's most dependable allies. Thus, although Reinhold Neibuhr may be upset justifiably by the rhetorical goings-on in the White House, he is ill-advised to base his critique on legal grounds:

> We do not know the architectural proportions of Bethel. But we do know that it is, metaphorically, the description of the East Room of the White House, which President Nixon has turned into a kind of sanctuary. By a curious combination of innocence and guile, *he has circumvented the Bill of Rights' first article.* Thus, he has established a conforming religion by semiofficially inviting representatives of all the disestablished religions, of whose moral criticism we were naturally so proud.[8] (Emphasis added.)

Richard Nixon, it would seem, not Madlyn Murray O'Hair or Reinhold Neibuhr, best understood America's rhetorical history. Richard Nixon knew, as Benjamin Franklin knew, that rhetorical engagements normally lie well beyond the arm of the law. The Bill of Rights placed very few sanctions on the rhetorical behaviors of worshipping presidents. Indeed, no matter what the separationists may claim, Richard Nixon's Sunday services abided by both the letter and the spirit of the First Amendment as regards rhetorical matters. As Robert Bellah has stated, "the separation of church and state has not denied the political realm a religious dimension."[9]

While some scholars may be unwilling to distinguish so readily and so sharply between the legal and the rhetorical components of church-state separation, most Americans seem generally to be nonplussed by the whole matter. Americans have allowed, for example, their Continental Congress to ingest "God or one of the numerous synonyms of the Deity into most all of its documents and promulgations," but they have demanded that "the Constitution emerging from the Convention [contain] no such invocation or reference."[10] As Leo Pfeffer once observed, "The omission was not inadvertent; nor did it remain unnoticed."[11] "Let religion and religious politicians have their rhetoric," reason most Americans, "but don't force us to sign loyalty oaths, require us to join an established church, or demand that we recite prayers in public schools." As long as organized religion is armed exclusively with rhetorical weaponry on the political battlefield, most Americans appear willing to reaffirm the covenant described by Sidney Mead:

> . . .(since the public welfare was to set the limits even of religious freedom, and the public welfare is a matter for the state to define) the way was left open for the state, if and when it judged that the religious sects were inadequate or derelict in the matter, to defend itself by setting up the institutions or machinery necessary to guarantee the dissemination and inculcation of the necessary beliefs. . . . The free churches accepted, or had forced upon them on these terms, the duty and responsibility to define, articulate, disseminate, and inculcate the basic religious beliefs essential for the existence and well-being of the society—*and of doing this without any coercive power over the citizens at all, that is, armed only with persuasive power.*[12] (Emphasis added.)

The rhetorical nature of the church-state compact in America is perhaps seen in sharpest relief when we look at the interesting nexus between the legislative and the rhetorical. In 1956, for instance, Senator Styles Bridges of New Hampshire introduced a bill which called upon Americans to "perpetuate renewed observance throughout the world, by nations and individuals, of the Ten Commandments."[13] As Paul Blanshard notes, since such a resolution would only be emotionally (i.e., rhetorically) binding on Congress, it was assumed that, were the resolution to pass, no one would test its constitutionality.[14] Essentially, of course, the bill called for nothing more than renewed rhetoric on behalf of the American civil religion, and hence, little concern was voiced over its potential to compromise church-state separation. Thus, although Bridges' motion adhered most closely to the tenets of the civil-religious compact (and hence was not likely to be questioned historically, philosophically, or legally), the affair was not without its procedural difficulties:

> When Bridges introduced his resolution in 1956, there was a moment of embarrassed silence while Senate officials pondered the question of which committee had jurisdiction over the Word of God and the Ten Commandments. Congress, of course, has no standing committee on the relations of church and state or the general extension of moral principles to world society. Finally, the Senate sent the resolution to the Committee on Foreign Relations![15]

Fluctuating Nature of the Contract
If I have left the impression that the "contract" was first written in the revolutionary era and has not changed a jot since that time, I have been misleading. Indeed, one of the most distinctive elements of the civil-religious-rhetorical covenant is the flexibility with which it meets changing exigencies. That is, while the quantity of "official" civil religious discourse may not change from age to age, the intensity with which America's national faith is preached, and hence the extent to which the terms of the contract are rigidly enforced, are quite variable indeed.

As we have seen in the early portion of Chapter 2, very real and very practical reasons prompted God and country to be conjoined rhetorically in the early days of this nation. With Britain's sabers rattling and with internal strife in the colonies continuingly imminent, the rhetorical power of organized religion was first unleashed on behalf of America and her aspirations for independence. The Reverend James Otis and his "black regiment" of colonial ministers "preached up" the Revolution "in innumerable 'fast day' and recruiting sermons."[16] Generally, however, they did so politely, not idolatrously; they were not mawkishly chauvinistic about their soon-to-be nation.[17] In any event, religion paid its rhetorical dues in colonial America, and later on, as Gribbin notes,[18] both Northerners and Southerners were treated to a passionate brand of "nationalistic" preachment by America's clergymen-patriots, before, during, and after the Civil War. Too, as Ray Abrams laboriously details in *Preachers*

Present Arms, the American clergy carried and used rhetorical machine guns when striving to live up to the terms of the contract, World War I style. While Abrams specializes in the sensational, the following excerpt he quotes from a speech by the Reverend Charles A. Eaton may not be all that unrepresentative of war-time preaching in the early 1900s: "When [the spy] comes sneaking around with a bomb, don't say 'Let us pray,' but take him out there on the marsh and tie him down and place the bomb on his chest. Light it and stand off and watch him blow to his Kaiser—to Hell! Be regular he-men."[19]

The contract has not always been honored with such intensity, however. Indeed, except for some World War I rhetoric, as well as that occurring during the "emotional spasm" of the Eisenhower years, Americans have become rather blasé about their civil-religious discourse. Sidney Mead suggests that this change in emotional tempo resulted from the burgeoning nationalism of post-Civil War America. Says Mead: ". . . American nationalism finally was rendered pervasive and secure by the Civil War. Just as the older Federalism disappeared in a new and unprecedented assertion of central power, the former dedication to the Union gave way to a novel but irresistible sense of organic unity. This nationalism no longer had the same need for the older mythic unity supported by religious sanctions."[20] Coupled with rising industrialization and the scientific era, America's nationalism could thus tilt its religious cap at a more rakish angle, the existential need for such rhetorical support having now passed.

My point, thus, is that there have been undulations in the emotional intensity of civil-religious discourse throughout America's history. This is not to say, quantitatively speaking, that the rhetoric has changed significantly. Today, for instance, our presidents still dutifully go through their religio-rhetorical paces, as do the clerical diviners who surround them at state functions. Yet as Paul Blanshard notes, the prayers of our congressional chaplains go almost totally unheeded, sometimes being delivered to a congregation of no more than six persons.[21] In contemporary times (as we shall see in Chapter 4), the pragmatic need for civil-religious discourse has been replaced by ritualistic exigence. Thus, while the terms of the contract are still adhered to "religiously," official civil pietists appear to do so out of habit, not out of burning, mandated conviction:

Despite all his elaborate staging, [President] Johnson's Prayer Proclamation got scant attention. It was lost in a whirlwind of activity—a stroll with his dogs around the White House grounds, luncheon at the National Press Club, supper for the Congress, signing other bills and proclamations (for example, "White Cane Day," October 15) and greeting callers like Sharon Moline of Salt Lake City, also known as "Miss Wool of America." The day ended, with a series of last minute conferences before driving out to the Naval Hospital in Bethesda for a gall bladder operation.[22]

Terms of the "Contract"

When reviewing the contract presented earlier, the reader's attention is directed to the three principles upon which this rhetorical compact is based: that religion can provide an ultimate meaning system for its adherents, that government is able to exert coercive influence on the affairs of its citizens, and that both government and religion wield considerable rhetorical power. By accepting such fundamental assumptions, the specific terms of the marriage contract become easier to see.

The first principle is perhaps the most subtle. Essentially, I am arguing here that organized religion serves to set a certain "tone" in America, a respect for faithfulness and an unblushing commitment to the ethereal, while government's day-to-day procedures make it seem an unimaginative, spiritless oaf. Government builds our roads, outfits us for battle, regulates our shipping, subsidizes our farms, computerizes our tax forms. Conversely, religion posits transcendent verities, takes a stand on other-wordly issues, discourses about the intangible, points us toward over-arching ethical standards, retrieves us from the miasma of ordinary existence. In short, religion gives us faith in faith. And when religion shares the motivational cosmos with government, it becomes only a short emotional step from faith to patriotism and from God to country—presuming, of course, that our political leaders have their rhetorical wits about them.

Thus, since many traditional western religions answer ultimate questions with some degree of authority and provide (through their respective eschatologies) a sense of destiny and purpose for their believers, it is small wonder that governments have so ardently courted such well-dowered mates. Too, religious bodies have usually been insightful enough to reckon with the awesome power which the state incarnate possesses—power to fill the state's coffers, to send its sons off to war, and to punish crushingly those who refuse to do so. Government, for all of its attractiveness, is a brawny, stubble-faced suitor. Finally, it must be remembered that the philosophical power of religion and the coercive influence of the state are buttressed equally by their ability to use rhetoric often and well. Indeed, the two combined may well constitute the most important rhetorical institution in the contemporary United States (much to the dismay of such spurned rhetorical rivals as black power, feminism, consumerism, and so forth).

But if organized religion and the United States government have joined together in holy rhetorical wedlock, the relationship promises to be a curious one: marital roles are carefully proscribed and prescribed; a sharp imbalance in power exists between the newlyweds; and, cruelest cut of all, the marriage cannot be announced in the local papers. Though she may have made an honest man out of Sir Government, Madam Religion lost more than her virginity on that fated day in 1787 when Preacher Franklin tied the knot for all eternity.

The Guise of Complete Separation
Thomas Jefferson notwithstanding, the American people have never witnessed a total bifurcation between its government and its religions. Franklin Littell makes the case more precisely:

> That men of different religious covenants may live together as good fellow citizens is a fact—and also a profoundly important theological event. It means that the religious covenants and the political covenants are separated. And that is the first phase of the guise of the American experiment—not "separation of church and state" (a misnomer, for we have *never* had it) but separation of the religious and political compacts. Our theoretical understanding has not, as yet, caught up with our experience.[23]

Surely, of course, government and religion have had their respective duties and influence in the United States, a set of conditions which many commentators would describe as "the genius of the American experiment in the disestablishment of religion." Still, although both of the contracting parties willingly agree to maintain the fiction of separation, God and government are enwrapped in each other's arms continuously, as Ms. O'Hair so exhaustingly details (here presented in modified fashion):

1. The United States government is especially liberal with regard to copyright requirements for religious publications.
2. The U.S. Office of Education publishes a booklet entitled *The Declaration of Independence and Its Story* which acknowledges the hand of God in the fashioning of the American republic.
3. Religious services and prayer breakfasts are frequently held in the White House and in other governmental buildings.
4. Congress has proclaimed April 30 the National Day for Humiliation, Fasting, and Prayer.
5. Congress has incorporated such organizations as the Boy Scouts and the Veterans of Foreign War even though such groups require belief in God for full membership.
6. Military chaplains, who perform a wide variety of religious functions, are salaried by the United States government.
7. The phrases "In God We Trust," "Under God," and "So Help Me God" have been legislated into official governmental language.
8. Catholic hospitals receive federal funds and yet refuse to perform legal abortions for taxpayers.
9. California gives state employees three hours off with pay for the observance of Good Friday.
10. The United States Department of the Interior and the United States Department of Agriculture permit church groups to hold religious services in national parks and recreation areas.
11. Texas school boards often inquire whether or not applicants for teaching positions believe in a Supreme Being.[24]

Naturally, this is only a partial listing of the numerous, often significant, interrelationships the United States government shares with organized religion. However, eminent students of religious freedom, such as Leo Pfeffer, could respond with an equally long list of principles and practices which *separate* God and Caesar:

1. There is no national religion which requires the membership of the American people.
2. Job discrimination on the basis of one's faith has severe punishments attendant to it.
3. No frankly religious precedent may be employed in the adjudication of a case in a court of law.

4. Prayer in the public schools has been banned.
5. Federal and state assistance to religious educational
institutions—as religious institutions—is prohibited.
And so on and so forth.

As Littell, Bellah, and O'Hair would argue, however, the separationists' case is primarily a legal one, not a sociological one. Or, as I would have it, not a rhetorical one. That is, the rhetoric of governmental officials is often openly religious in tone, as we have seen in Chapter 1. At the same time, nevertheless, the very same governmental spokesmen will claim, paradoxically, that this is an areligious country where persons of all (or no) faiths are treated equally under the law.

As is so often the case with rhetorical perplexities, both sides are right—we are a legally areligious people but we are also ardent admirers of civic piety. Notice, for example, that of the eleven "violations" O'Hair points up, only two (numbers 8 and 11) are totally bereft of a rhetorical dimension. Numbers 2, 3, 4, 7, and 10 refer to rhetorical-ceremonial concessions government has made on behalf of religion—proclamations are issued, public space is made available, religious language is added to public rituals, and God is mentioned occasionally in governmental documents. Notice, too, that few funds are expended on behalf of such activities, that there are no concomitant legal sanctions imposed, and that an aspect of compulsion is nowhere present in the above-cited infractions. Finally, it should be remembered that sentimental forces (e.g., number 1), traditional forces (5), psychological forces (6), and political forces (9)—not binding legal ones—have motivated most of the other violations O'Hair has mentioned.

All of this is not to say that rhetorical violations do not run counter to the spirit of the First Amendment or that there are no existential violations of its letter in the United States today. Nevertheless, because the American people have managed to fashion a legal disestablishment, and have replaced it with the rhetorical trappings of a civil-religious polity, they have maintained the alternative that all human interactants have—that of not listening to each other.

The Guise of Existential Equality
"It is distinctive of our country that we have developed a relationship in which church and state can cooperate without the

one dominating the life of the other: government not dictating to the church; and the church, on the other hand, not dictating to government."[25] Thus opined the Reverend Oswald C. J. Hoffman when, in the early 1960s, he addressed the Pentagon Protestant Pulpit, a weekday series of noon-hour services conducted by members of the clergy in the Concourse of the Pentagon. In this section, we shall see that the Reverend Hoffman was half right: the church does not dictate to government.

Of all the charges that can be leveled at the American civil religion, the most strident is that our national faith is an agent through which the dignity and prophetic spirit of religion is sapped. According to such a perspective, American religion unwittingly has agreed to a contract that even a first-year law student would find degrading and manipulative. American religion is being used, argue such persons, used for the greater honor and glory of the United States government. As we shall see later in this essay, these commentators are largely correct.

Before getting into such polemics, however, it is well to survey the facts in the case. Are religion and government existential equals? Had both parties reached the existential age of consent when signing their John Hancocks (and Johnathan Edwardses) to the contract they devised? The answer to both questions is clearly no. While the church in contemporary society has significant (largely rhetorical) influence over the lives of its adherents, it does not possess the coercive, adjudicative, tax-making power of its contractual partner. The church's realm is clearly the rhetorical—it can make words about social conditions and governmental priorities but it cannot enforce its will directly and immediately as can government. This is not to disparge the power of discourse, for, as the United States government knows full well, the rhetorical influence of the churches earmarks them as one of its most prized allies. Yet, when government can require even conscientious objectors to fight in its wars, when government can make laws relative to tax-deductible religious contributions, and when government can compel the churches to insure that their buildings conform to health and fire codes, it is clear who wields the existential club, as has been rather sardonically pointed out by sociologist Bernard Bell:

> Certainly no competent sociologist or political scientist, no scholarly observer of our country who is not himself a professionally

ecclesiastical person, says or thinks that the Church has much to do with the complexion of the contemporary American picture. Instead, their usual conclusion is that most Americans regard the Church as promotor of a respectable minor art, charming if it happens to appeal to you, its only moral function to bless whatever the multitude at the moment regards as the American way of life.[26]

Things were not always so, of course. In the early days of our country, the church had considerable rhetorical *and* existential power. But as historian Alan Heimert notes, things began to change in the nineteenth century:

To be sure, the campaign of 1800 clearly marked the beginning of a more secular era in American politics. With it began an era in which the lay orator, rather than the preacher, increasingly took over the task of expounding public issues for and to the popular mind. . . . But in the aftermath of the war, the clergy seemed to retreat into a self-imposed ecclesiastical exile, thus completing a transition that had begun, even before the war, with the rise of lay spokesmen to eminence in American political life.[27]

At this point apparently, the existential-rhetorical balance began to shift. The roles of the contracting "parties" became more sharply defined; job descriptions were written; and the coordination of religious rhetoric and governmental action was effected. To the dismay of some, organized religion thus became a rhetorical lackey—indoctrinating the tribe's warriors as they went out to battle,[28] providing a "spiritual embellishment" and a "useful sustaining force" to governmental policy,[29] and generally becoming a potent, albeit suasory, factotum in American life. As Will Herberg sadly notes:

In this reversal the Christian and Jewish faiths tend to be prized because they help promote ideals and standards that all Americans are expected to share on a deeper level than merely "official" religion. Insofar as any reference is made to the God in whom all Americans "believe" and of whom the "official" religions speak, it is primarily as sanction and underpinning for the supreme values of the faith embodied in the American Way of Life. Secularization of religion could hardly go further.[30]

While theologians may well cringe at such a set of conditions, the American church probably effected the very best deal possible. Unbalanced though the contract was, it was a contract nonetheless, with significant dividends accruing both to the greater and to the lesser of the two "equals." Since, as Loren Beth indicates, the church did "not contain all of the citizens of the state, and therefore [did] not have jurisdictional rights coextensive with those of the state,"[31] it grabbed for the most it could—rhetorical jurisdiction. The church reserved the right to advise, to admonish, and often to advance governmental policies and behaviors, and the state agreed to provide a very public forum for the espousal of mainstream civil-religious viewpoints.

Thus, the genius of the compromise must not be understated. Because of it, church leaders were accorded rhetorical access to the heads of state, allowed to set the agenda for discussions of the various moral issues affecting the American government, and generally treated with respect, if not obeisance. Rather than incorporate church in state, with all of its attendant abuses, and rather than relegate the church to third-class status, the American people permitted religion to occupy an honored place in the national sun. By carefully modulating the existential/rhetorical balance between church and state, Americans thereby avoided the Scylla of irreligiosity and the Charybdis of pure theocracy.

As a conclusion to this section, it might be helpful to consider the alternatives the American people had to institutionalizing civic piety, to *not* agreeing to the contract I am attempting to explicate in this chapter. Loren Beth provides a handy summary (here modified for brevity's sake) of the various church-state options confronting our colonial choosers:

1. Pure theocracy—a situation in which actual political authority is held and exercised by the heads of the ecclesiastical establishment.
2. Total separation—complete and unalterable separation of church and state.
3. Mixed theocracy—the state is regarded as subordinate, even in temporal affairs. It is allowed such autonomy as the church is willing to grant it.
4. Total identification—a situation in which every citizen is subject to the state, politically, as well as to the national church.
5. Total conflict—often witnessed in quasi-totalitarian countries, this is a system in which church and state aggressively attempt to vanquish each other.

6. Erastianism—a condition in which the state is accorded control of religion in order to secure religious peace, thereby establishing a national religion.
7. Totalitarianism—a situation in which organized religion is totally vanquished by the state and where the opportunity for religious observance is denied.
8. Partial separation—most commentators see this as the American system, in which the dignity and jurisdiction of both church and state is respected by both parties.[32]

When placed in such a perspective, the rhetorical-contractual situation I have been describing here seems less than far-fetched. After all, history had shown the colonists that total separation was impractical for a nominally religious people, mixed theocracy not feasible for such a diverse citizenry, total identification and pure theocracy philosophically repugnant for a people attempting to escape such systems, and total conflict and totalitarianism un-acceptable on any reasonable grounds. Which left partial separa-tion . . . and erastianism.

From the rhetorical-existential imbalance we have seen in this chapter, and from the features of civil-religious discourse we shall observe later in this essay, it appears that the American people happened upon a church-state system even more curious than that of partial separation—*they created a kind of rhetorical erastianism in which the state was granted existential jurisdiction over its citizens (and their various religious institutions) and the church allowed to share in the rhetorical jurisdiction over the American people.* Concomitant with this arrangement was an agreement to maintain the fiction of total separation through the agency of civic piety.

Naturally, there are those who might argue that I have been much too cavalier when characterizing church-state relations in America as rhetorically erastian. There are those who might argue that religious groups have dragged government (kicking and screaming, often) into certain arenas of social reform. And there are those who might argue that as a result religion has *not* become government's existential lackey. Nevertheless, it seems obvious that government, not religion, has effected or retarded social reforms on a national scale. While it is important to note that government's ear has been bent by religious groupings in such matters, it is equally important to remember who has done the urging and who has done the acting throughout America's social history.

Maintaining Rhetorical Balance

With the twin proposition the "First party (government) rhetoric will refrain from being overly religious and second party (religion) rhetoric will refrain from being overly political," we come upon the most important feature of the contract I have been describing in this chapter. Most governmental spokesmen and religious leaders attempt a rhetorical juggling act when dealing with politically tinged religious issues or with affairs of state bordering on the theological. The rhetorical ideal, of course, is to maintain the hyphen in civil-religious matters.

The delicacy with which church and state treat each other is pronounced. During the tribulations (and later, trials) of Watergate, for instance, mainstream American churches generally circumnavigated the matter. Although some civil-religious pagans (like the Reverend Peter Christianson) passed out petitions among their congregations which called for the impeachment of Richard Nixon, "moral outrage from the pulpit was not as widespread as it might be."[33] John Cardinal Krol, Roman Catholic prelate to Philadelphia, "skirted any specific mention of Watergate, lumping it with other evils as part of 'a serious departure from ethical and moral principles.'"[34] Also, when American Episcopalians gathered for their triennial general convention in Louisville in October of 1973, they failed to go on record regarding Watergate. Even groups as disparate as the Christian Church (Disciples of Christ) and the Union of American Hebrew Congregations failed to issue a strong statement on Watergate. The American civil religion, it would appear, is a fair-weather religion with regard to the political scene.

By and large, it has always been so. As rhetorical scholar Harry Kerr indicates, even the fast and thanksgiving sermons preached in colonial times were uncharacteristic of the usual rhetorical fare served up to the colonists: "Published sermons indicate that ministers seldom forsook Christ for long, and even if the political enthusiasm of an occasional minister caused him to neglect his religious role, at least he retained an audience. Considered in this light, fast and thanksgiving sermons present the *rare* picture" of the colonial preacher.[35] Alan Heimert appears to agree with Kerr when he remarks that "with the exception of John Davenport (and, for a few years in the 1680s, Increase Mather and his fellow critics of moderate government) few New England preachers had publicly stood as spokesmen *against* the standing order."[36]

This being the case, the pacifist preacher is an especially interesting character. Like his fellow ministers, he is obliged by the terms of the contract to refrain from being excessively political. If politics must be mentioned by him, his remarks should reaffirm the standing political order. Those pacifist preachers during World War I who refused to abide by the terms of the contract met with a number of unfortunate circumstances: some were despised for disobeying "the tribal gods"; most were barred from their pulpits; some were never able to find another pulpit; and others gave up the ministry entirely.[37]

It is this matter of excessive concern for political matters which most clearly helps us to discriminate among the rhetorics of "official" and "unofficial" civic piety. When a religious rhetor discourses on political matters, he often relinquishes his claim to the rhetorical dividends accrued by those who follow the straight and narrow. Rabidly political (especially, anti-establishment) preachers are quite rightly feared by national, state, and local government officials who seemingly realize that such persons are doing violence to the contract and thus upsetting the rhetorical applecart. On the other hand, excessive establishmentarianism by religious leaders is also feared by politicians and viewed with a jaundiced eye by the electorate. It is because the normative constraints on religio-political discourse are so tight, therefore, that we find the following tale to be amusing: "Father Taylor during an exciting election campaign once prayed, 'O Lord, give us good men to rule over us, pure men who fear Thee, righteous men, temperate men, who—pshaw, Lord, what's the use of veering and hauling and boxing around the compass? Give us George N. Biggs for governor.'"[38]

Needless to say, the rhetorical sword cuts both ways. Just as we demand that our preachers keep their politics to themselves, so too do we require that our politicians be religious—but not too religious. Politicians must thus walk a rhetorical tightrope, paying proper homage to America's God, but avoiding being gushy about it. In 1972, for example, George McGovern took great pains to "hide the fact (and ban the photo) of himself as pastor of a

Methodist church,"[39] even though he did, of course, make occasional theological allusions in his speeches. Similarly, both Presidents Johnson and Nixon were careful not to identify "Vietnam policy with the designs of God in whom Americans professedly trust."[40] As Richard Neuhaus declares, such a rhetorical gaffe "would have occasioned a severe conflict between the churches and American civil religion and inflamed a public debate about 'the purposes and meaning of our beloved nation'" which would have been both "intense and corrosive."[41]

The archetypal dilemma faced by American politicians was revealed in the candidacy of John Fitzgerald Kennedy. After all, Kennedy belonged to a church which is often seen as embarrassingly public in its religious professions. The ornateness of Catholic architecture, the ostentatious nature of traditional Catholic services and ceremonials, and the clannishness and ethnicity of Catholic worshippers all conspire to depict them as capital-R religious. In contrast, as Alley points out, the American civil religion has been largely Protestant in design and execution since its inception.

Thus, while sociologists and political scientists may argue that it was the essence of Kennedy's Roman Catholicism which frightened the American voter in 1960, it seems just as reasonable to suggest that it was the *rhetorical manner* in which Catholicism is traditionally displayed that made them suspicious of a Kennedy presidency. Catholicism, with its traditional claims to theological supremacy, its non-egalitarian private schools, and its mysterious religious formulas, has typically given only grudging respect to the American civil religion. Apparently aware of such attitudes and prejudices, Kennedy himself displayed a tasteful but somewhat cavalier attitude toward religion, ostensibly attempting to manifest rhetorically his concern for abiding by the civil-religious contract:

> Some have termed John Kennedy a "spiritually rootless modern man." Others have spoken of him as a secular man. These references point to his unwillingness to adapt himself to institutional religion. JFK accepted religion as a part of his life, but his closest associate, Ted Sorenson, could say: "But not once in eleven years —despite all our discussions of church-state affairs—did he ever disclose his personal views on man's relation to God." Sorenson also informs us that Kennedy cared "not a whit for theology." He apparently saw the Bible as a good source for quotations, but with

no more reverence than he might have had for other great literature, and possibly less than he had for Jefferson. As one historian phrased it, he "wore his religion lightly."[42]

Whatever he may have felt personally, John Kennedy did his utmost to respect the terms of the public contract his forebears had signed.

The Future of the "Contract"

That I have been discussing the weighty matters of God and patriotism with the spiritless and mercantile metaphor of legal contracts may offend some readers. The hushed, reverential tones with which Robert Bellah speaks of his civil religion surely has greater poetic and spiritual value than does my humble image. I hope to have shown, however, that figuratively speaking, the American government and organized American religion have made a deal, a transaction based on the division of existential and rhetorical roles. I have suggested that civil-religious discourse can best be understood if we keep in mind this contract and its constituent parts. In arriving at this contractual metaphor, I perhaps have not drawn on the better tendencies of humankind, as has Robert Bellah. But I have drawn upon very human instincts nonetheless, instincts rooted in a canny, practical understanding of how a country must be simultaneously religious and areligious for it to function properly. In thereby demythifying some of the rhetorical discourse we prize most as a people, I have attempted to avoid debunking it, although I have grounded my understanding in the rough-and-ready, thoroughly practical, and willingly rhetorical nature of the American people. That Americans have chosen to maintain a collective fiction of church-state separation, while at the same time reverently draping their national icons with religious vestments, is hardly condemnatory, no matter how paradoxical it may appear.

As we approach the latter part of the twentieth century, however, there is growing evidence that the contract will be honored with less zeal in the future. Already, we are beginning to see growing ecclesiastical concern over the imbalance between the contracting partners. For example, when "Cardinal Spellman of New York described our armed forces in Vietnam as 'soldiers of

Christ' and declared himself in favor of 'my country right or wrong,' he was severely censured by most of the religious press."[43] Similarly, although the Clergy and Laymen Concerned About Vietnam were composed of, at best, 10 percent of the American clergy, [44] the very existence of the group indicates that some are chafing under the constrictions of the contract. Also, with ministers, priests, and nuns now being elected to state and national offices, there seems to be some sentiment to rid the country of the rhetorical erastianism I have alluded to earlier. Moreover, we are now hearing the voices of many theologians who decry civic piety, voices which ask for a more telling and demanding civil-religious rhetoric, indeed, even voices which demand less talk and more action. As the voices grow louder and more insistent, and as more and more clergymen demand to renegotiate the contract, it is conceivable that many will heed the warning that Franklin Littell issued in 1962:

> If "the American religion" continues to emerge, bringing with it the hearty and uncritical affirmation of everything American, the time may yet come when believing Jews, Catholics, and Protestants will have to face up to tribal religion in its more demonic form. In that day they will learn, as has been learned by the religious remnants who have remained faithful in the face of other totalitarianism, that they have much in common besides a goodly land.[45]

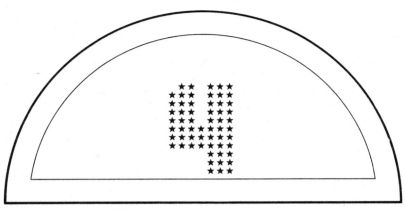

The Rhetorical Properties of American Civic Piety

The rhetoric associated with American civil piety is a complex thing. As we have seen, such discourse derives its rationale from a potpourri of human motivations. Too, its manifestations are as variable as its authors are numerous. Yet, when treated as a body of rhetoric, civic piety is revealed as containing a rather distinctive and consistent pastiche of elements, even though it is fueled by personal predilections, to be sure.

To a large extent, the rhetoric of the American civil religion has become—in our times, at least—what Kathleen Jamieson would call generically calcified.[1] That is, it responds more surely to its own "antecedent rhetorical forms"[2] than it does to the peculiarities of the exigences to which it responds daily. Frederick Fox has pointed out, for example, that proclamations issued by American presidents on our national days of prayer are distinguished more by their similitude than they are by the unique rhetorical personalities of their creators. It does not take a cynic, implies Fox, to note the isomorphic qualities of Kennedy's and Eisenhower's proclamations:

> Eisenhower: "This Nation, under God, arrived at its present position by the toil and sacrifice of many citizens who subordinated personal interests to the common welfare . . . in the unconquerable spirit of a free people . . . to work toward goals of human betterment which may be attained only beyond our span of years."

Kennedy: "This Nation under God has achieved its great service to mankind through the toil and sacrifices and subordination of personal desires to common welfare, . . . in the unconquerable spirit of a free people . . . to work for goals of human betterment that lie beyond our span of years."[3]

That a Catholic Democrat should borrow so faithfully from a Protestant Republican in preparing his remarks reveals both the universal nature of the American civil religion as well as the inventional constraints willingly observed by its spokesmen. The story of civil religiosity in America is a story which has been told many times previously in the pages of rhetorical history—a story of the substitution of commonplaces for *topoi* as aids to rhetorical invention, of speakers' dependence upon stock phrases rather than ideas developed for the unique communicative situation at hand.

In this chapter, we shall look rather carefully at what appears to be the distinguishing aspects of civil-religious discourse. We shall attempt to see whether Gabriel Fackre's phrase, "the musak of civil religion,"[4] is an accurate (or needlessly precious) description of American civil piety. More specifically, we shall examine four features of civil-religious discourse which provide it with its distinctive, even formularly, flavor. I shall argue here that civil-religious discourse in America is characterized by its expedient complexity, its non-existential content, its ritualistic presence, and its prosaic animus. Although such traits appear to accord themselves with Fackre's "musakal" description, we shall see that no facile designation of syrupy mechanism is alone able to capture the essence of rhetorically enlivened civic piety.

Expedient Complexity

Expediency

Although many commentators have accused politicians and clerics alike of dallying venally with civic piety, rhetorical facts marshalled in support of such charges have been few and far between. For at least one American politician, Richard Nixon, such allegations of religious opportunism seem to be partially justified.

Having collected a sample of 201 public speeches delivered by Richard Nixon between 1948 and 1974, I proceeded to search each address for civil-religious themes. Keying exclusively on references made to America's "God(s)," I found that 28 speeches (18 ceremonial, 10 non-ceremonial) of the 201 contained god-references, while 173 did not. Of the 56 god-references, 12 were in introductory portions of the speeches, 9 in middle segments, and 35 in the concluding remarks.

It does not take a rigorous statistician to see to the core of Nixon's rhetorical inclinations as regards matters theological. Less than 14 percent of Nixon's speeches contained divine allusions. Of the fifty-six identifiable references made to (or about) God by Nixon, thirty-five (or 62.5 percent) were found to reside within his perorations. Of the remaining references, the majority were used by Nixon to pry open his addresses. Equally interesting is that there appeared to be no easily discernible chronological pattern to Nixon's deployment of the heavenly hosts. Rather, Nixon mentioned God selectively throughout his career, his choices apparently being dictated exclusively by the demands of the rhetorical situations he faced.

Almost 65 percent of the speeches containing theological refrains emanated from ceremonial situations. Three of the speeches were eulogies, three were convention acceptance addresses, three were remarks made at religious gatherings, two were State of the Union Addresses, two were holiday proclamations, and, of course, two were his presidential inaugurals. The remainder were commencement addresses, remarks made at memorial dinners, and election day speeches.

Of the ten non-ceremonial addresses, four were "crisis" speeches (on Vietnam, on Watergate, and on the economy), four discussed the "communist problem," one was a campaign speech (delivered in 1974), and the last was an instance of the "One America" speeches Nixon gave from time to time during his rhetorical career. It is particularly noteworthy that almost none of Nixon's theologically embellished speeches dealt avowedly with partisan politics, welfare, higher education, international diplomacy, the natural environment, or other work-a-day vicissitudes of American life. For Richard Nixon, at least, God was a rhetorical comrade to be relied upon infrequently but dramatically.

Although others may argue to the contrary, there is little reason to suspect that Nixon's rhetorical choices relative to God were singular. He, like most American presidents, was a nominally religious person. Reared a Quaker, Nixon revealed a modest and decorous respect for America's politico-religious heritage throughout his public life. As we shall see shortly, Nixon's rhetorical behavior was rather typical of his political predecessors and, conceivably, of his successors as well.

Complexity
Naturally, no mere quantitative description of civil-religious rhetoric will suffice to explain its suasory rarefractions. Rather, it is the content of the civil pietists' remarks which provides us with the best understanding of the phenomena I am attempting to describe here. More specifically, it is by attuning ourselves to the pantheon of Gods which (ostensibly) guides and sustains the American civil religion that we can discern most clearly its theological essence as well as its rhetorical methodology.

It will be remembered that when Robert Bellah first remarked about the American civil religion, his data base was generated largely from the maiden speeches of America's presidents. While Bellah has stimulated a wealth of research on the topic, no scholar, curiously enough, has returned to examine the initial sources of many of Bellah's insights. Therefore, a systematic examination was made of each of the forty-seven presidential inaugurals with a rhetorical eye being peeled for the kinds of gods mentioned by the chief executives. The results are as fascinating as they will be, for some, disturbing.

America's Gods: Numerous observers have remarked about the "God who guides this great and good nation." Such comments oftentimes have embraced a full measure of outrage: "The 'God' referred to [in patriotic messages] is only an abstraction, a digit in political computations, a football in political maneuvers."[5] More cerebral commentators have been equally concerned with two questions: Does America have one God or many Gods? Upon what theological axis does America's God(s?) turn?

In response to the first question, Robert Alley relates a story about arch civil religionist Billy Graham. During an interview, Graham was once asked: "What God, by your definition, would be equally acceptable to Jew and Christian alike?" Alley reports that "Graham was somewhat flustered when he responded with a question, 'Do you mean the God up there or the God in Christ?' He [Graham] became quite aggravated as he dismissed the questioner with obvious displeasure, passing to safer ground with another reporter."[6] Alley sees such a vignette as having significance for the American civil religion: "Of course, Graham is not a dualist in his views, he does not believe in two Gods, and he was using a figure that snared him. Nevertheless, he was asserting what amounted to a dualism, which he regularly affirms on occasions when he moves from his 'Hour of Decision' to a White House Prayer Breakfast. Billy Graham is only one of many evidences of a burgeoning national cult in the United States."[7] As we shall see, Graham—as a civil pietist—is neither a monotheist nor a dualist. Rhetorically, the apologists for civil religion in America are polytheists of the first order.

As for the characteristics of America's God(s), a number of designations have been offered, the most cogent, perhaps, being that put forth by Bellah himself: "The God of the civil religion is . . . on the austere side, much more related to order, law, and right than to salvation and love. Even though he is somewhat deist in cast, he is by no means simply a watchmaker God. He is actively interested and involved in history, with a special concern for America."[8] That Bellah associates a multiplicity of facets with America's God suggests that a conception of active polytheism may provide for us the most fertile understanding of America's theological sovereign. A careful examination of rhetoric expended on His (or Their) behalf helps to document such a notion.

The American Pantheon: Bellah, of course, was right when he asserted that each American president has utilized the Lord as a solemn footnote in his inaugural address (save one—a brief one—Washington's second). What Bellah did not report, but what a systematic inspection of the inaugural addresses reveals, is that in the forty-seven inaugurals (Ford's address at his swearing-in ceremony being considered an "inaugural" for our purposes), numerous and varied descriptions of America's God are presented. Of the 183 descriptions of the deity offered by our presidents, five general themes (or "Gods") emerge. These include:

1. *God the Inscrutable Potentate*—This is a powerful and protective God, one who oftentimes, but mysteriously, directly intervenes in the affairs of Americans. According to Washington, He is powerful—the "Invisible Hand which

conducts the affairs of men."[9] According to Jackson, He is also protective of the nation-state; He is the "Power whose providence mercifully protected our national infancy." According to Grant, He is rather arbitrary as well, one who "in His own good time" would make war-torn America one again. And according to Lincoln, one who had much experience with this mysterious, oftentimes fickle God who seems to delight in caprice, His succor would be garnered for America when "God Wills" it in "His appointed time." Thus, God the Inscrutable Potentate is a God to be reckoned with, but he is equally a God with whom it is difficult to know how to reckon. He is, according to McKinley, a cosmic wheeler-dealer: "[God] will not forsake us so long as we obey his commandments and walk humbly in His footsteps."

2. *God the Witnessing Author*—Here in our pantheon we find the Creator God who authors things both human and divine and watches His creations from afar. This is a silent, onlooker God, a non-participant in human affairs. He was, for George Washington, the "Great Author of every public and private good," and for Polk, He who fashioned our democratic form of government. He is an "ever-watchful" God who looks "down upon us all," one who is an especially obliging witness to our national ceremonials. According to some of our presidents, God the Witnessing Author is the *deux ex machina* for our national social apparatuses.

3. *God the Wise and the Just*—This is an increasingly popular God in our national pantheon, one whose counsels and ministrations provide a reservoir of knowledge and justice for humanity. He is a Receptacle God from whom presidents and preachers alike draw their human portions of wisdom. This is the God who provided Franklin Roosevelt with "Divine guidance," the God who watched over Taft in the "Discharge of [his] responsible duties," and the "Almighty Providence" who helped Herbert Hoover handle the "ever-increasing burdens" of the White House. In addition to dispensing wisdom, this is a God, too, who became John Adams's "Fountain of Justice" and Lyndon Johnson's rather stern, Old Testament-like overseer: "God is harshest on those who are most favored." However, from the standpoint of the inaugurals, at least, God the Wise and the Just was a

rather reluctant wellspring of justice, rarely threatening His minions in LBJ's style. More often, He contented Himself with enlightening the minds of His servants and left the business of justice to more human agencies.

4. *God the Genial Philanthropist*—This is a rabidly partisan deity. God the Genial Philanthropist dispenses both material and emotional gifts to the deserving, and the blessings of His Providence have often been recounted by America's chief executives. Unlike God the Wise and the Just, this is an active God who dispenses prosperity (five times in the inaugurals), wisdom (five), strength (four), peace (three), mercy (two), and freedom (two references). This divine assortment of benefits has accrued uniquely to Polk's "Heaven-favored land." According to Ulysses S. Grant, His munificence has even included the most tangible of bounties: "providence [has] bestowed upon us a strong box in the precious metals locked up in the sterile mountains of the far West. . . ."

5. *God the Object of Affection* —Only occasionally can God the Object of Affection be seen in the inaugural rhetoric of America's chiefs of state. This is a God who deserves, but who does not demand, expressions of love and obedience from His faithful. Only in the occasional remarks of the more contemporary presidents, however, do we find anything resembling a full-bodied declaration of gratitude to this rarest of America's Gods. Harding, Truman, FDR, Eisenhower, and Nixon (repeating FDR verbatim) have briefly expressed the nation's gratitude to and affection for God. Most of the presidents have concentrated instead on initiating or renewing their bargains with the Lord, rather than thanking Him for services rendered or promising Him future obeisance.

These, then, are America's Gods. That they are mentioned but briefly by our chief executives is probably less important than the fact that they are mentioned at all. And their relative popularity should not go unnoticed. Below, we find some indication of the collective rhetorical weight they have been accorded by the presidents in their inaugurals.[10]

Deity	Percentage of Times Mentioned		
	All Inaugurals	Early Inaugurals[a]	Later Inaugurals[b]
God the Inscrutable Potentate	33.5	45.4	21.0
God the Witnessing Author	17.1	14.1	19.9
God the Wise and the Just	16.1	8.6	24.3
God the Genial Philanthropist	28.6	29.7	28.2
God the Object of Affection	4.7	2.2	6.6

[a] From Washington's first through Cleveland's first (roughly the first half of the inaugurals).

[b] From Cleveland's second through Ford's swearing-in speech.

As might be expected, God the Inscrutable Potentate and God the Genial Philanthropist led the field during the earliest inaugural addresses. Most presidents, however, have sampled equitably within America's pantheon (with the exception of God the Object of Affection). Of all the presidents, Washington, Lincoln, and Eisenhower made the greatest number of references to the deity, while ten of the presidents made but one allusion to God. No president chose to mention all five of the Gods being described here and most appeared to have had a "favorite" heavenly consort (e.g., in his second inaugural, Lincoln focused special attention on God's inscrutability).[11]

Some interesting temporal differences are revealed in our quantitative analysis, however. The apocalyptic God (which understandably captured Lincoln's attention) appears to hold less interest for our contemporary presidents. Balancing that is a growing rhetorical concern for the wisdom and justice of God, perhaps reflecting a decreased fascination with the God of the Old Testament, perhaps reflecting nothing more than personal choice. Most likely, however, such a shift of heavenly emphasis reflects a growing confidence in America's ability to solve her own problems, a confidence which precludes the necessity of a transcendent God. A receptive God, an inactive God, a "font of wisdom" God may well be on its way to becoming America's most popular God. And unless the trend reverses itself dramatically in the future, it appears that God the Object of Affection—the God who receives—will continue to be shunted aside for Gods less obviously self-centered.

Several conclusions seem warranted by our brief examination of presidential rhetoric:

1. America's God is multi-faceted, containing numerous (sometimes competing) traits.
2. America's God is not vengeful, nor does He typically punish those who transgress His laws.
3. America's God is, by and large, a passive God whose name is invoked *after* America has set its sights in a particular direction.
4. America's God is more an immanent than a transcendent God, one who reinforces America's political destiny and becomes our stalwart companion during our national trek.
5. America's God is man-centered; man—"in his individual and corporate being—is the beginning and end of the spiritual system of much of present-day American religiosity."[12]

Above all, America's God is not an object of divination for America's presidents. Our politicians do not attempt to discover the "will and intention of the gods, and thereby to foretell the future, or explain past events."[13] Rather, "God is conceived as man's 'omnipotent servant'"[14] by many of our civil pietists. At least as presented rhetorically, America's God is an expedient God, one who watches over us as we set about our various national tasks. Moreover, He is a complex God, who provides a multitude of inventional resources upon which *civil* religionists (and, sometimes, civil *religionists)* can draw. Finally, He is an expediently complex God whose pieces and parts are so intricate, so plentiful, and so delightfully contradictory that they can provide rhetorical support for any number of sainted or diabolical schemes.

One final note of caution. In opting for my polytheistic explanation, I have been operating exclusively on rhetorical grounds. That is, my inspection of presidential rhetoric has revealed that five different Gods (or, at the very least, five quite different features of the same God) have been employed as rhetorical helpmates by America's chief executives. This is not to say, naturally, that the American people "really believe" that their national destiny is guided by a heavenly quintet. It is to say, however, that these are the Gods who have been introduced to the American people on a quadrennial basis.

Conclusions: While such expedient complexity may hold a fascination for the rhetorical or sociological scholar, there are many who decry its philosophical and theological implications. Senator Mark Hatfield, for one, has lashed out bitterly at such rhetoric. Speaking at the National Prayer Breakfast in February of 1973, Hatfield told the members of his audience (one of whom was Richard Nixon) that, the rhetorical efficacy of America's Gods notwithstanding, serious moral implications inhere in the usual brand of civic piety: "If we as leaders appeal to the god of an American civil religion, our faith is in a small and exclusive deity, a loyal spiritual Advisor to American power and prestige, a Defender of the American nation, the object of a national folk religion devoid of moral content. But if we pray to the Biblical God of justice and righteousness, we fall under God's judgment for calling upon His name, but failing to obey His commands."[15]

Non-existential Content

In suggesting that the content of "official" civil-religious rhetoric is non-existential, I am suggesting that an active, behavioral concern for the tangible exigencies of the moment is not generally characteristic of such discourse. Rather, civil-religious discourse of the official stripe busies itself with the past and the future more than it does with the present. Additionally, such rhetoric is richly symbolic, reveling in a world of images rather than with practical policy. That such characteristics distinguish official civil-religious discourse from its (comparatively tawdry) unofficial brethren seems undeniable. That such features comport themselves with the contract as outlined in Chapter 3 also seems true.

In unpacking the parts of the proposition offered above, we shall examine the quiescent, nostalgic, and millennial emphases to be found in much official civic piety. As we progress, it should be remembered that it is primarily the non-existential content of such rhetoric which has come under attack by the detractors of the "American civil religion." From my vantage point, however, it is its non-existential character which has allowed it to function at all in American society.

Quiescent Nature
When the 1976 bicentennial celebration of the American republic was being planned, many of its architects in Washington feared two things: that the churches of America would not participate in

force (thereby insuring the failure of the national celebrations), or that the churches would participate in untoward—that is, in activist—ways. In my lexicon, it was feared that American prelates would not uphold their halves of the contract, and that the activism which swept through even establishmentarian churches in the sixties would continue apace, thus insuring no (or, worse yet, an untraditional) civil-religious commemoration. In short, it was feared that America's preachers would become exhortative rather than rhetorically reactive.

But there was no need to worry. In detailing his bicentennial suggestions for the Church of the Covenant, for example, Joe Williamson admits that such non-contractual thoughts had run through his and his colleagues' minds:

> Early in our conversations about the possibilities of this event we became convinced of the importance of disassociating ourselves from the "official" Bicentennial programs which are devised in Washington. Those programs are being set up to reinforce the tendencies of "civil religion" in America. That form of religion weds the religious rhetoric of faith to the policies of the political establishment and seeks to sanctify those policies in the name of God. We felt it of paramount importance to do just the opposite. We affirmed the need for a new "declaration of independence," specifically a declaration of independence by the churches from the state.[16]

However, after waxing on in this same article about the church's historical position on such matters, Williamson concludes with a rendition of the bicentennial plans finally adopted by the Church of the Covenant:

> We have begun to develop an alliance with other religious people who share our sense of things. We have developed a funding proposal which will provide money to help us carry out our plans. We would like to help other churches recover their sense of history as well. These histories will be written into pamphlet forms which can be distributed to visitors who come to Boston during 1975-76. We also intend to create a series of dramatic and artistic presentations which tell the story of our past and call us to respond faithfully to that past in the present. Street theatre, multimedia, music, mime, and dance are all being explored as ways to do this dramatic representation. We would also like to construct a major convocation in the city of Boston which will call for the intersection of religious vitality and political commitment.[17]

Thus, despite the temptations of libertarian thought, Williamson's church, at least, has opted for the historically sanctioned course in such matters—completely symbolic, non-activist events. The contract continues.

Most American churches followed suit. The Baptists, for instance, sponsored a series of sermons on the topic "Let Christ's Freedom Ring," assemblies and programs on the bicentennial themes, pageants, dramas, and choral work celebrating America's history, the publication of local church histories, bicentennial "heritage" rallies, and a sedentary-sounding Christian Citizenship Workshop whereby "church members [can] become more actively involved in the processes of government."[18]

The Baptists, of course, are not alone in sponsoring such quiescent, largely symbolic events. (Nor are they to be censured, unless, of course, one advocates substituting action for rhetoric and the complete overturning of the contractual applecart.) Even the American Jewish community—hardly a group reluctant to act out its strongly felt religio-political beliefs—contented itself during the bicentennial with preparing a portfolio of drawings by Mark Padwal depicting highlights of the American Jewish contribution during the last two hundred years, a series of lectures on Jews in American society, as well as myriad other symbolic activities.[19]

The preparations made for our national celebration by religious groups serve as models in high relief of the usual sort of rhetorical fare served up by civil religionists. The religio-political establishment in America is, as we have seen in Chapter 3, one founded upon a bedrock rhetorical assumption—that blatant political activism by the churches or the refusal by government to participate with the church in dialogue are eventualities to be eschewed. If the American civil religion is a religion (and, as we have seen, there is little reason to suspect that it is), it is a rhetorical religion. As a "religion," it does not take verifiable action. It does not give alms to the poor. It does not even hold bingo games. Rather, it is a religion which exists within and because of discourse. Since it *does* nothing it is doomed to tag-along status existentially. On the other hand, it owes its very preservation to the fact that it *does* nothing. For, when ritualistic rhetoric becomes something other than ritual, it too must open itself up to the scrutiny, actions, and potential rebuffs of all who inhabit the marketplace of controversy. For the theological establishment in America to operate non-rhetorically (i.e., existentially) in civil-religious matters would be to lose the very tangible benefits which accrue to faithful handmaidens of government.

That civil-religious rhetoric is designed not to have existential import is revealed notably in our national documents. Kendall and Carey, among many others, have noted that the *existenz* of legal proclamation will have no part of a church-state, no matter what that state will permit on more patently rhetorical fronts:

> The Declaration of Independence, with its references to the Creator, to the laws of nature and of nature's God, to Divine Providence, appears to be the declaration of a religious people, of, more specifically, a *Christian* people. The Constitution and the Bill of Rights, by contrast, have in them not one word that could not have been written, and subscribed to, by a people made up of atheists and agnostics. The Declaration seems to be the declaration of a people who wish to make clear above all else their commitment to work the will of God; the Constitution and Bill of Rights seem to be the expressions of a people whose exclusive concern is with the things of this world.[20]

Not all of us, it would seem, are willing to acknowledge the reality and worth of the subtle but crucial distinctions made by our forebears between the existential and the rhetorical. Alarmists such as the Veterans of Foreign Wars have worried needlessly about the existential import of the Supreme Court's decisions relative to church and state: "If we were to drop God from our vocabulary we would have quite a job. How would we do it? Would we take a razor blade and cut 'God' from our Bibles? Must we eliminate the mention of God in our Declaration of Independence, Pledge of Allegiance to the flag and in our national anthem? Must we destroy all money on which appears the words 'In God We Trust?'"[21] While the VFW may well see this "derhetoricalizing" as an ominous sign indeed, they surely miss the genius of the civil-religious contract when reasoning to their conclusion: "If we go to these ridiculous extremes we might as well finish the job by closing all the churches, imprison [sic] their spiritual leaders and follow [sic] the communists' adoration of Lenin."[22] Fortunately for the civil-religious establishment in America, cooler heads have been able to separate existential reality from rhetorical reality throughout the republic's history.

It equally distorts the contract, however, to argue from rhetorical premises to existential conclusions. The Reverend Joseph Costanzo, a Jesuit apologist for greater state aid to religious institutions, typically bases his arguments on rhetorical grounds:

> Wholly in accord with this original corporate and unofficial profession of the religious foundations of American democracy are the individual official pronouncements of the highest government officers from the very beginning of the Republic. To discount the long tradition of presidential utterances, especially the presidential Thanksgiving Day proclamations, as expedient and pious exhortation is to testify to the strength of the American consensus that the nation's religious foundations must be officially acknowledged and promoted.[23]

The typical reply made to such charges is akin to that of disestablishmentarian Leo Pfeffer: "Government expenditures of tax-raised funds for religious institutions cannot easily be justified on the basis of . . . meaningless acts of ceremonial obeisance." [24] Although Pfeffer's contention does indeed have both practical and historical sanction, he has surely underestimated the considerable power of public rhetoric when he terms its manifestations "meaningless."

All of this is not to say that to act rhetorically is not to act at all. In Austin's terms, civil-religious rhetoric is performative.[25] That is, the very fact that the Church is accorded rhetorical status equal to that of government *is* an existential affirmation of the worth of church-state harmony in America. For clerics and statesmen to share the speaker's platform during our bicentennial celebrations was to continue to work out a very old and very necessary rhetorical compromise. Were the church to imbed existential punch into its rhetoric by calling, say, for Congress to redistribute America's wealth, it would be dallying unadvisedly with a rather workable rhetorical compact. Little is really lost, argues the civil-religious lobby, when those at the United States military academies are compelled to attend chapel. For, as United States Solicitor General Erwin Griswold has remarked, "no cadet or midshipman is required to believe what he hears."[26]

Containment: The natural, rhetorical result of the bifurcation I have been describing between the suasory and the existential is one that I touched on briefly in Chapter 3. The civil-religious

discourse emanating from America's clergy is, by and large, ac-
comodationist rhetoric, a rhetoric tacitly supportive of the political
status quo. It functions to legitimize the current political order, a
task much unlike that performed by many revolutionary era
preachers who used their pulpits to preach all manner of sedition
against the British.

In post-revolutionary times, however, the established church
in America has demonstrated a particular genius for ascertaining
by whom and on what side the national bread was being buttered.
Conrad Cherry explains such rhetorical accomodation in the most
pragmatic of terms: "It is now a sociological and historical truism
that any religion which becomes a vital part of its culture is inclin-
ed to maintain the status quo of that culture. When the motifs of
the national faith are invoked, therefore, it is frequently for the
sake of uncritical endorsement of American values and tasks."[27]
According to Wallace Fisher, such syncretistic behavior runs
directly contrary to the sectarian ideologies built up by many
religions over centuries of activism: "civil piety and religion-in-
general blur the particularistic genius of the Reformation and
Catholic traditions."[28]

Perhaps Fisher is right, but he has failed to reckon with the
politically unsavory alternative of failing to legitimize the current
national ethos—that of being relegated to insignificant rhetorical
status. For all of his fulminating, Billy James Hargis (a most unofficial civil religionist) has obtained small access to the corridors of
power in Washington. By paying their rhetorical dues, however,
and by delicately bringing to bear the considerable collective influence they have, establishment prelates consistently hold open
the possibility of modulating the socio-political environment.
Whatever the philosophical costs of tacit legitimization—and its
tacitness should not be forgotten—it is the only politically astute
game in town, as has been pointed out grudgingly by Fox:

> Even though he [the President] invites preachers of different faiths to
> speak in the White House—distinguished Catholics, Jews, and
> Protestants—they all tend to bring him the same message. Few would
> dare to criticize him under his own roof as Nathan the prophet
> once criticized David the King for sending a soldier to death in
> combat so he could have his wife, Bathsheba. Nixon's clergy never
> criticize him for sending bombers over North Vietnam. They
> mainly come to encourage and inspire.[29]

It is for these and other similar reasons that we find no truly prophetic God in America's civil-religious pantheon. No God of Abraham opined during our bicentennial celebrations. Rather, God becomes what Andrew Greeley calls a "senior partner" to American interests,[30] a God whose rhetorically necessary immanence precludes Him from having a viably transcendent voice. In civil-religious terms, America's God is a God who watches the American people as they march their leaders in and out of office. The realities of power being what they are, He could not be otherwise, lest He be made to reside in generously taxed churches. Apparently, such a set of conditions has never been attractive to the American people. Hence, the contractual beat goes on.

Those who denounce this accomodationistic God of the American people (as manifested in civil-religious rhetoric) too often forget that—in societal terms—there are many other rabidly prophetic Gods inhabiting the rhetorical marketplace. While our national God may tacitly sanction "the massacre of Indians, . . . the lynching of Blacks, . . . the atom-bombing of Japanese, . . . [and] the napalming of Vietnamese children,"[31] it cannot be forgotten that there were many other Gods speaking out all the while, Gods who were true to their denominational heritages. It cannot be forgotten either that we are talking here about a *national* God, one who is conjured up rhetorically by a veritable cacophony of priestly voices. Finally, it should not be forgotten that the contract has never been as one-sided as many of its detractors would have us believe. Government needs its religion-tinged rhetoric just as surely as the church needs the tangible benefits of governmental affiliation. As Peter Berger has observed, "Religion legitimates so effectively because it relates the precarious reality constructions of empirical societies with ultimate reality."[32] Thus, while its content may have few activist implications, civil-religious rhetoric is an imperfect but reliable guardian of the very existential relationship shared by church and state in America.

The Curious Case of Doctor King: When commenting upon an earlier draft of this manuscript, a colleague of mine strongly objected to what seemed to be a rightist bias implicit in my analysis. He argued, for example, that a person like Martin Luther King, Jr., stood in sharp contrast to the accomodationists I have been describing in this essay. King, with his mass marches, his sundry civil disobediences, and his fitful exhortations surely does not—at first glance—appear to fit in with the non-existential phenomena I have been describing thus far. Following such a line of reasoning to its natural conclusion, one might suggest that King's conception of a highly judgmental God (who smiles kindly on social activism) clearly gives the lie to my analysis.

The most obvious response to such an argument is also the least satisfactory: Martin Luther King, Jr., was clearly an anomoly in the pages of civil-religious history. A more telling retort might be that King, for all of his reverence for God the Wise and the Just, never completely severed the bonds between himself and the political establishment in Washington. Most important of all, King was a member in good standing of the rhetorical establishment. It is not an accident of history that King is best known for his "I Have a Dream" *speech* and his *letter* from the Birmingham jail. Nor is it wise to forget that preacher King used public discourse as the focal point for almost all of the civil rights demonstrations he engineered. And it is important to remember that the Black Power movement was launched by those who sought to fill in the behavioral-existential void created by King's willingness to effect change through *rhetorical* agencies.

Naturally, had he lived, Doctor King would have objected strenuously to the quiescent bicentennial celebrations. Nevertheless, it is hard to imagine that he would have failed to participate in them. It is equally certain that he would have found some way of breathing rhetorical fire into the nation's festivities. Thus, while King may have rejected much of the civil-religious contract, it seems clear that he respected its underlying rhetorical essence.

Nostalgic Nature

Perhaps because it has now become a rhetorical institution in America, civil-religious discourse tends to turn in upon itself; it tends to use its own ancestral rhetorical forms to provide itself with both a rationale and psychological momentum. As we shall see, civil piety is largely antiquarian.

In 1954, William Lee Miller observed that the faith of Americans "is not in God but in faith; we worship not God but our own worshipping."[33] In a similar vein, I am suggesting here that civil-religious discourse is *meta-rhetorical* since it typically discourses about kindred remarks made previously. If there is a civil religion in America, it is not a faith in faith (as Will Herberg would have it). Rather, it is a faith in *statements* about faith, faith-in-faith as rhetorically pronounced.

Most religio-political rhetoric—of both the official and unofficial varieties—exhibits such meta-rhetorical features. For example, the Christophers, an association of Catholic laymen, has published a widely distributed tract entitled, *Every President Invoked God's Help*.[34] The eight-page pamphlet is little more than a random collection of religious remarks made by America's presidents. What is most interesting is that, except for a two-paragraph introduction, no original material appears in the pamphlet. It is as if invention relative to civil-religious themes had been sapped long ago by the Christophers, as if there were no longer any pressing, existential need to create remarks capable of meeting ongoing rhetorical circumstances.

Such meta-rhetoric has its obvious benefits for civil-religious spokesmen: (1) it facilitates rhetorical invention by eliminating the need to search potential *topoi,* allowing such speakers to depend on ageless, previously articulated themes instead; (2) it provides its authors with a certain sense of security because it grounds itself in rhetorically innocuous precedent; (3) it helps to raise the emotional impact of the discourse since it revels so totally in the hallowed past, thereby remythifying the civil-religious compact; and (4) most important, perhaps, is that such an approach discounts the use of inventional materials and myths derived from denominational or politically partisan underpinnings. All of these benefits, no doubt, add to the heart-warming glow of the heart-warming glow described by Clarence Manion:

> There is a heart-warming glow around the conjunction of "God and Country." The expression stirs the stimulating sensation of patriotism down to and through its deepest roots. At Gettysburg, Lincoln prayed that "this nation, under God" might have a new birth of freedom, and in saluting the American flag today, we all repeat the declaration that this nation shall stand, "under God, with liberty and justice for all."
>
> This conjunction of God and Country runs like a bright golden thread in and throughout the entire fabric of our political and constitutional history.[35]

The meta-rhetorical nature of much civil-religious discourse also reveals its strongly cosmological overtones. Unlike much contemporary discourse, religio-political rhetoric continually looks to its beginnings when attempting to explain (or to explain away) contemporary vicissitudes and challenges. It draws its strength from its revolutionary roots, even though it often distorts those roots in a salad of querulous historical allusions. Like any cosmological rhetoric, it "defines the power of the supernatural, guides human behavior, provides a system of norms with ethical implications, and upholds and sanctifies the values of society,"[36] by gorging itself rhetorically in days gone by. Thus, it comes as little surprise that we find a certain breathy quality to the pages of *The Military Chaplain:*

> If our Bicentennial is to be a true celebration of 200 years of our history, and a springboard to a "New America," a "New Spirit of '76," all the national, statewide, city and village organizations and plans underway to mark that anniversary and to make America live anew, vibrant with hope and opportunity, had better "look back" and remember that God has been a part of our history since our founding and, undoubtedly, the source of the manifold blessings this land has enjoyed.[37]

According to Philip Hammond, such rhetoric raises "to hagiologic stature the persons thought to have conceived and instituted the [democratic] procedure: the Washingtons, Jeffersons, and Lincolns."[38] An understanding of the cosmological nature of civil-religious rhetoric allows us to understand why, of the three main bicentennial themes—Heritage '76, Festival '76 and Horizons '76— it is the first that has received the overwhelming attention of America's religious leaders. Perhaps because the oblique lessons, personae, and myths of yesteryear are not likely to rise up to contradict statements made today, the past is a comfortable (for many, an emotionally compelling) receptacle of public thoughts. Rhetorically speaking, then, Ezra Taft Benson has chosen well when exulting:

> Let us not permit these admonitions of our living prophets to fall on deaf ears. Let us, as they direct, learn the meaning and importance of our God-ordained Constitution. Let us rededicate ourselves to the lofty principles and practices of those wise men whom God raised up to give us our priceless freedom. Our liberties, our salvation, our well-being as a Church and as a nation depend upon it. This nation has a spiritual foundation—a prophetic history. Every true Latter Day Saint should love the United States of

America—the most generous nation under heaven—the Lord's base of operations in these last days. May we do all in our power to strengthen and safeguard this base and increase our freedom.[39]

Millennial

Besides rushing pell-mell into the hoary arms of the past, civil-religious spokesmen often skirt the *existenz* of the moment by speaking in millennial terms. Many observers trace the millennial themes to be found in civil-religious discourse to ideas first set afloat during the Great Awakening. While some scholars have suggested that a messianistic conception of America was in no way that of Johnathan Edwards,[40] the notion of America as a Redeemer Nation was made popular during his time. As Sydney Ahlstrom notes, the millennial concern "was on men's minds on the first Fourth of July, and in somewhat more secularized form it would become an enduring feature of American patriotic oratory."[41]

Whether because of its Judaeo-Christian roots or because of its prideful people, America has often pointed to a Golden Age when she would lead the world's children out of darkness. In an excellent essay, J. F. Maclear has traced millennial themes throughout America's history and has found them to be one of the most abiding features of its national consensus.[42] In revolutionary times, sermons of the ilk of "The American States Acting over the Part of the Children of Israel in the Wilderness and Thereby Impending their Entrance into Canaan's Rest" (preached by Nicholas Street in 1777),[43] served to set the millennial tone. Later, according to Maclear, the most successful years of postmillennialism in America were those between 1815 and the Civil War, but even during Reconstruction the millennial theme continued to compel the American people.[44] Too, Ray Abrams credits much of the success of the pro-World War I rhetoric of America's clergymen to its millennial urgings.[45]

In relatively modern times, we sometimes find the Children of America's Israel on the march once again. Note, for example, the particularly virulent messianic strain found in the rhetoric of Harry Truman:

> . . . Religion should establish moral standards for the conduct of our whole nation, at home and abroad. . . .
>
> For the danger that threatens us in the world today is utterly and totally opposed to all these things [spiritual values]. The

international Communist movement is based on a fierce and terrible fanaticism. It denies the existence of God and wherever it can it stamps out the workshop of God. . . . Our religious faith gives us the answer to the false beliefs of Communism. . . . I have the feeling that God has created us and brought us to our present position of power and strength for some great purpose.[46]

Although millennial attitudes may compel contemporary Americans as individuals, these stark public themes (of a virtuous people leading its lesser brethren to some previsioned eschaton) appear to have become a bit too rich for our increasingly cosmopolitan rhetorical blood. Such trumpetry is being replaced in religio-political discourse by a kind of demythologized pragmatism, a belief that the nation's destiny has already been assured by dint of social technology. Thus, while futuristic themes still tend to distinguish civil-religious discourse, the messianistic motifs of the Great Awakening have been replaced in recent times by more urbane rhetorical goals.

Conclusions: Whatever it has become, however, civil piety continues to eschew rhetorically the travails of the present. As we have seen, its most typical religious proponents assiduously avoid embracing activist, policy-oriented themes. We have observed, too, that civil-religious discourse focuses largely on the past and the future. Thus, when he resigned the vice-presidency, Spiro Agnew's humiliation did not preclude him from demonstrating his diligence as a student of civil-religious rhetoric:

> But I can't help thinking tonight of James Garfield's words to an audience in New York just following the announcement that Lincoln had died. Garfield, who was later President himself, was only a young Army officer at the time of that great tragedy in 1865, but he saw clearly where his country's strength lay, and he expressed it all in these few words to a frightened crowd. He said: "Fellow citizens. God reigns, and the Government in Washington still lives."
> I take leave of you tonight, my friends, in that same somber but trusting spirit. God does reign. I thank Him for the opportunity of serving you in high office, and I know that He will continue to care for this country in the future as He has done so well in the past.[47]

Ritualistic Presence

Much of what has been said thus far undergirds our conception of civil piety as ritualistic. As we have seen, there is a certain sameness to the divinities invoked in such discourse; there is a tendency to resort to civil-religious themes on official occasions exclusively; there is a marked avoidance of the vicissitudes of the moment. In all of this, one unmistakable impression emerges: civil-religious discourse is animated by and finds its fullest expression in ritual. For many reasons, the rhetoric of the American civil religion is a rhetoric forged by political necessity, tempered by religious pluralism, and polished by ritual of a most public sort. It is, according to Duane Litfin, "a kind of periodic tipping of the hat to God to appease Him; a sort of national knocking on wood."[48]

Ritualistic Forms

In their simplest forms, rhetorical rituals do two things: they resolve ongoing exigences (e.g., the need for commemoration) in stylized ways and they provide a familiar, collective vehicle for the expression of certain powerful human emotions. By accepting these twin functions as those native to ritual, we can see why civil piety has reveled in ritual almost since its beginnings in the Thanksgiving and Election Day sermons of colonial America. The religious experience, says Thomas O'Dea, is "spontaneous and creative"; institutionalizing that experience through rhetorical ritual reduces "these unpredictable elements to established and routine forms."[49] Such routinization makes for predictability, for the sure knowledge that God is in His sky and watching over the American people. That these thoughts have to be rekindled from time to time through ritual does not gainsay the depth of such sentiments. In fact, it is the functional repetitiveness of civil-religious discourse—the God Day Rallies, the Washington Prayer Breakfasts, and the Fourth of July services—which keeps the religio-political machinery in this country well oiled and operational.

Ritualistic Events: Civil-religious discourse clothes itself in the garb of rhetorical ritual in primarily one of two ways. The first is the ritualistic event, in which the entire rhetorical interaction is posited on civil-religious premises. The tabernacle, the congregation, the deacon, and the sacred scriptures of nationhood are intertwined in such a way that no other outside exigence is dealt with. On such occasions and in such places, God and America receive the top and only billing.

These ritualistic productions are often large-scale affairs. Take, for instance, the God Day Rally sponsored in 1973 by the Catholic War Veterans of Brooklyn. The Veterans announced their event in an upbeat manner: "Plan God Day Rally at St. John's University in September, Ten Thousand Expected to Attend." "With the blessing and prayerful endorsement of Bishop Francis J. Mugavero of the Brooklyn Diocese," the event was heralded as one "paying homage to God and allegiance to Country through a Prayer Rally and special patriotic observances."[50] The dignitaries at the God Day Rally included leaders of the church and of civic and governmental groups, as well as a congressman (Lawrence J. Jogan, R. Md.—the sponsor of the "Human Life Amendment" in Congress).

The color and pageantry expected at such events was amply provided by the United States Army Band, the Young Americans Drum and Bugle Corps, the St. Agatha Glee Club, St. Ephrem's Choir, and the Patron Nations' Festival Dancers. The highlight of the celebration was a "God Day Mass" concelebrated by numerous dignitaries of the Church. Thereafter, an assortment of civil-religious activities were administered by fifty religious leaders (of countless religious persuasions) and "forty lay-leaders of civic, patriotic, veteran and pro-life groups."[51] A parade through the university's grounds and a prayer rally provided the capstones for the three and a half hour affair.

Such a brobdignaggian production is not atypical. Especially during the bicentennial celebrations, extended ritualistic events were the rule rather than the exception in hamlet and city alike. That thousands upon thousands of persons would willingly drench themselves in such religio-political oratory probably says as much about their regard for the inherent attractions of collective celebration as it does about their fervor for linking the temporal and the divine. "Those who would dismiss the sacred ceremonies as mere antiquated conventions, and the rhetoric of ceremonies as an insincere attempt to marshal the support of pious people," claims Cherry, "would miss the cultural significance of these occasions of worship."[52] They would miss, too, the colorful continuity provided our civil religion by the agentry of dramatic ritual.

Ritualistic Themes: The less histrionic and more common manifestation of civil-religious tenets is the passing reference found in political and religious oratory. Inaugural addresses, invocations, benedictions at political rallies, and the like are the rhetorical workhorses of civic piety in America. As we saw in Chapter 1, the pervasiveness of such ritualistic themes is so unquestionable a part of public rhetoric in America as not to be noticed. While such themes do not normally prick the collective consciousness as vividly as does the ritualistic event, they do serve to remind us inexorably of our dual obligations to God and Caesar.

As we have seen in the case of Richard Nixon, certain ground rules must be observed when deploying such themes: (1) they must be brief, (2) they must commence or terminate an address (but usually not both), and (3) they must normally (i.e., during peacetime) be appended to ceremonial, as opposed to policy-making or policy-endorsing, speeches. According to some, these rhetorical stringencies denude religion: "God, says the unwritten glossary of American politics, is a word in the last paragraph of a political speech."[53]

We have seen, however, that such ritualistic themes and rules were not fashioned for the sake of liberal theologians or effete academicians. While God may well be a cosmic afterthought in American political rhetoric, He *is* present, no matter how tattered and ill-fitting His costume may appear to some. The utilization of religio-political themes by groups such as the American Legion is as much an affirmation of popular sentiments as it is a reflection of our insatiable human need for pageantry: "[Local Legion posts] are urged to close Communion Breakfasts, Post Installations, etc. with the following but simple ceremony to give greater glory to God and a greater respect for our country. Use simple birthday candles and at the close of the gathering have everyone light them and hold them above their head. The person in charge of the gathering shall lead or choose someone to lead the people in the song, 'God Bless America.'"[54]

Rhetorically speaking, the rigidifying of civil-religious events and themes carries with it certain liabilities. With sameness, after all, can come somnolence. The following vignette of the National Day of Prayer, Eisenhower-style, illustrates the point well:

When October 2 arrived, it turned out to be a dud, at least as far as public praying was concerned. The President saw this first hand. He attended a special morning service in his local Presbyterian Church and was very disappointed by the turnout. As he said afterwards, he found himself praying among "only a handful of people."

When he returned to the White House, he began an immediate investigation; that is, his secretary phoned me to find out what had gone wrong. Why had the Day been so poorly observed?

I [his consultant for religious affairs] immediately got State on the phone and asked them to tell me why. They assured me they had mailed the President's August 8 proclamation "to fifty major religious press services and periodicals." Many of these had reprinted the text in full but, as I said earlier, the popular press gave it scant notice. Even the Presbyterian churches neglected to use it in their Sunday bulletins. It simply had zero grass roots appeal.

As I reported this to the President, he gritted his teeth. He did not like to be beaten on any front. If the Congress required him to proclaim an annual Day of Prayer, he was determined to have it heard the length and breadth of the land.[55]

On the other hand, the alternative to *not* regularizing civil-religious events and themes is quite unattractive: "The only other possibility [for scheduling the National Day of Prayer] would have been to save it for the best crisis of the year. . . . But then, the proclamation might become more un-nerving than inspiring; the people might await its annual issuance with some dread."[56]

Such problems notwithstanding, ritual does seem to "work." But contrary to what Costanzo feels, ritualized civil-religious discourse has not "set an incontrovertible historical record of the religious presuppositions of our national existence and endurance."[57] Rather, such rituals serve to reinforce, to revivify, and to resanction the rhetorical convenant made by church and state decades ago. Naturally, when the American people find the contract to be attractive no longer, they will urge their religious and political leaders to abrogate the agreement and to overturn the sort of rhetorical edifice described in this chapter. What is more likely, however (given the rather dire consequences of such a decision as outlined in Chapters 2 and 3), is that the American people will continue to appreciate their religio-political rituals.

And the suasory power of ritual should not go unnoticed. "It does not matter that we are a practical and sophisticated people, no longer (we think) influenced by symbols, myths, or rituals,"

argues Michael Novak.[58] We do respond to such rhetorical entreaties and we do reject would-be presidents should they not
measure up to our ritualistic standards:

> Eugene McCarthy is quick to see through and to deflate the American
> civil religion, its rituals and its deficiencies. . . . Even astute
> commentators have been unable to understand McCarthy's refusal to
> believe. *They* believe. His agnosticism affronts them. They called
> him lazy, moody, irreverent, unpredictable, irresponsible, not
> serious, a poet, a dreamer. Whereas, in fact, he is merely
> hard-headed, a skeptic, who refuses to accept the rituals, to confess
> the mysteries, to pretend to the powers. [McCarthy once said] . . .
> "Take the magic out of it. I'll take the issues before the people.
> That's all it takes." He was wrong, of course.[59]

Ritualistic Features
Shortly after he became America's thirty-third president, Richard
Nixon initiated a series of weekly worship services in the White
House. Because the services were held in the White House, and
because they were of a religious nature, the American civil
religion was thus given a ritualistic shot in the arm on a biweekly
basis. The program detailing the service of June 29, 1969, is particularly instructive:[60]

June 29, 1969

Prelude
Opening Remarks   The President
Doxology
Prayer   Dr. Louis Finkelstein
                         Chancellor, The Jewish Theological
                                    Seminary of America
                                         New York City
Hymn   "We Gather Together"
Anthem   Members of the Christ Lutheran Church Choir
               "Now God Be Praised In Heav'n Above"
                                   by Melchoir Vulpius
                            Director: Mr. Geoffrey Simon
Hymn   "O God, Our Help in Ages Past"
Benediction
Postlude

We see here the same sort of ritualistic structure described earlier. We see, too, a certain theological anomoly. In commenting on the White House services, columnist Edward Fiske remarked: "The nondescript nature of the liturgy that is followed was evident when no one saw any contradiction in asking Rabbi Louis Finkelstein, a chancellor of Jewish Theological Seminary and preacher on June 29, to stand by while the congregation said the Doxology in praise of the Christian Trinity."[61]

In the remainder of this section, I shall attempt to explain why a Jewish rabbi was able to participate gracefully in a nominally Protestant service. Such an understanding will derive from the proposition that the level of abstraction imbedded in civil-religious discourse is so high that even obvious contradictions can reside peacefully under its sacred canopy (to borrow Peter Berger's happy phrase).

Having observed that civil-religious discourse is largely ritualistic and non-activist, we can easily understand its abstractness. It should be noted, however, that its abstractness does not render it incapable of eliciting rather concrete responses from the American people. Rather, civil piety depends upon its devotees to ferret out precise understandings of its moral implications.

Not all scholars would agree with such a statement, however. Robert Bellah himself seems to have observed a great deal of specificity in the pronouncements of the American civil religion. He implies, for example, that a sentence fragment from Kennedy's inaugural ("the revolutionary beliefs for which our forebears fought") contains a rather explicit suggestion that America should be about the business of solving its "greatest domestic problem, the treatment of the Negro American."[62] Bellah also suggests that Kennedy's exhortation that God's work be our own work is an explicit, "very activist and non-contemplative conception of the fundamental religious obligation, which has been historically associated with the Protestant position. . . ."[63]

While there is little doubt that John Kennedy's sympathies lay with the black American, and while it is reasonable to assume that many Protestants could find favor with Kennedy's inaugural address, the specificity discovered in Kennedy's remarks by Bellah could also have resulted from an unconscious attempt by a Berkeley sociologist to validate his own understanding of America's "self-understanding." Surely the phrase, "God's work must truly be our own," could, if uttered by Richard Nixon, be seen as yet another Republican plea for decentralizing the federal government and for increasing the economic determinism of the individual American.

The position to be taken here, then, is that most civil-religious discourse is highly abstract . . . and necessarily so.[64] Moreover, I shall argue that such abstractness serves three very pragmatic functions, all of which dovetail with the contractual metaphor used to explain the existence of civil piety in Chapter 3.

Symbolic Unification: One of the inescapable facts of our nation's history is that we have been a theologically pluralistic society for some time. Even in the homogeneous (by contemporary standards) society of revolutionary America, civil-religious discourse functioned to integrate the diverse religious affiliations of the colonists and to fashion from them a political consensus. According to Winthrop Hudson, for example, the earliest version of religio-political discourse in America paid its inventional debt to the Old Testament, suggesting, perhaps, that symbols capable of unifying various sectarian interests were desired even then: "This faith of the new republic was neither sectarian nor parochial. Its roots were Hebraic. Its explication was cast in Hebraic metaphors—chosen people, convenanted nation, Egyptian bondage, promised land. Its eager millennial expectation was expressed in the vivid imagery of the Hebrew prophets."[65]

Contemporary civil pietists have learned their historical lessons well. The need for a symbolically "compact" and integrative religio-political patois, for a rhetoric around which all rabid denominationalists and partisan politicians could rally, presses upon us. According to Bernard Bailyn, religiously tinged rhetoric provides a "higher justification, a breadth, generality, and intensity,"[66] unavailable in patently political, non-abstract rhetoric. Because pluralism reduces "matters of ultimate commitment to matters of personal preference,"[67] the public rhetoric of the civil religion must be quietly evocative:

> "Service to God and Country" is basic Americanism. It is not a fostering of religious worship in order to appease any element of our citizenry or to draw attention from any less desirable social activities. Since it is essentially basic Americanism, it is strictly non-denominational, non-sectarian. It is not intended to act

independently of religious groups but to cooperate with them to the end that the American people might never forget that God is the source of all their rights and privileges.[68]

On this same score, Murray Edelman has suggested that when one person uses a phrase like "governmental control" and another refers to "private enterprise," we learn "nothing from their speech about political economy but we do learn something important about the group values with which each identifies."[69] Similarly, to lace one's political speech (or religious sermon) with the metaphors and imagery of civil piety is to acknowledge one's allegiance to a national consensus without identifying the existential import that that consensus might have for oneself or for one's audience. Thus, there was little need for Rabbi Finkelstein to feel offended by the Protestant doxologists in the White House. They did, after all, speak the same language, a language shared by American Catholics as well:

> In his inaugural address Kennedy avoided the articulation of any specifically Roman Catholic doctrine or references to Jesus Christ and the Church. Participation in the ceremony was invited through appeal to such beliefs as "the rights of man" that come from the "hand of God." A similar, but less absolute, differentiation occurred in the funeral for Robert Kennedy. There specifically Christian doctrines were articulated, but the eulogies of both Senator Edward Kennedy and Archbishop Cooke dwelt mostly on civil religious themes. The upshot of the ceremonial differentiation between the civil religion and other American religions is that an American may be a Methodist, a Conservative Jew or a Roman Catholic and at the same time participate in the celebration of the civil religion—but without insisting that the civil religion be expressed specifically in Methodist, Jewish or Catholic terms.[70]

Ambiguous Delineation: Having observed (1) the non-activist themes to be found in civil-religious discourse, (2) the abstractness of its language, and (3) that "only 24 percent of American Protestants feel that it is right for clergymen to discuss political candidates *or issues* from the pulpit,"[71] we are left with an interesting dilemma: having ruled out so much, how is it possible for an official civil religionist to talk at all?

With calculated ambiguity. Rarely, these days, do we find the forthright language of Bishop Theodore S. Henderson of Detroit who, when addressing a Methodist conference at Atlantic City in

March 1918, urged his fellows to "get in touch with our War Council, should you find anybody of pro-German tendencies in your community. Let us locate, eliminate, and exterminate every pro-German in this country."[72] Such confessional zeal for the national religion is surely out of step with the normal rhetorical artistry exhibited by today's civil pietists. For example, in "specifying" what it means to "keep this a nation under God," the Christophers suggest that the shibboleth reminds us that:

—Men derive their rights directly from God.
—The authority of all government co.nes from the Lord by way of the people.
—The function of government, consequently, is to act as the agent of the people in securing their God-given rights and in promoting the general welfare.[73]

If this quotation typifies the optimum level of specificity to be found in official civil-religious discourse (and I believe it does), it is small wonder that such addresses are normally quite brief.

The ambiguity in civil-religious discourse is such that (according to Cherry) there probably never has been "a consistent meaning of [our] national symbols. . . ."[74] Even in revolutionary times, claims Harry Kerr, "it was fortunate . . . that the preachers avoided specific applications to current problems. Whatever such applications might have added to the interest and impact of the [Election Day] sermons would likely have been offset by the irritation of auditors who felt that they were being told how to conduct their business."[75] As Kerr is quick to point out, this reluctance to be specific was not characteristic of the ministers when they spoke on other occasions.

On the contemporary scene, however, prelates do not employ such situational specificity when discoursing on civil-religious matters. No matter what concrete referents words such as *church, state, establishment, free exercise,* and *separation* may have for some people, when imbedded in consecutive discourse by civil religionists they are made to dance to the tune of ambiguity. "Even the word *God*," says Sidney Mead, "had become so ambiguous long before theologians announced his death that the Federal Communications Commission was led to declare in July 1946 that 'so diverse are these conceptions that it may be fairly said, even to professed believers, that the God of one man does not exist for another.'"[76]

Mythification: Although the language of religio-political discourse is typically ambiguous, it is much more than that—it is richly ambiguous. That is, within its ambiguity it embodies conceptions of the national ethos grander than those which average Americans could articulate for themselves. The national myths allow the American audience to transcend the mundanities of day-to-day existence, making them part of a larger and more satisfying social enterprise.

It comes as no surprise, then, that the rhetorical energy of the American civil religion derives from its capacity to ennoble conception. The myths of a New Israel, of a God-fearing people, of strict separation of church and state, of the Holy War, and the like function as do all myths: "The myth, then, is a comprehensive view of reality; it explains it, interprets it, provides the ritual by which man may maintain his contact with it. . . ."[77] Thus, when terms like *freedom, democracy,* and *providence* lost their specificity for the American people, says Cherry, they actually increased their utility as conjurers of grand images.[78]

According to Irving Kristol, the mythification of life through rhetoric holds special appeal for the American people. As Kristol wryly points out:

> Just imagine what our TV commentators and "news analysts" would do with a man who sought elected office with the promise that, during his tenure, he hoped to effect some small improvements in our condition. They would ridicule him into oblivion. In contrast, they are very fond of someone like John Lindsay, who will settle for only the finest and most glowing goals. Public figures in our society get credit for their utopian rhetoric—for their "charisma," as we now say—and only demerits if they emphasize their (necessarily modest) achievements.[79]

Whether Kristol is right in his ethnocentric view of mythification is, of course, a matter for some debate.[80]

Perhaps no sub-theme in the catalog of civil-religious discourse has been mythified more richly than that of a bellicose America. Although he is too simplistic in arguing that World War I "back-the-war" rhetoric only had "to be couched in holy phraseology to bring forth the desired responses from the church people," the mythical themes reported by Ray Abrams are familiar and powerful ones indeed:

The Old Testament, with its war-god, Jahweh; the Holy Wars of the Israelites, the Imprecatory Psalms, and the Day of the Lord of Amos; the heathen in his blindness versus the Christian, the false versus the true gospel; the Christian crusades, the war hymns of the church; the example of Jesus driving out the money changers from the Temple and rebuking the Scribes and Pharisees; the sufferings of little innocent Serbia and Belgium and the cross of Christ, the symbol of sacrifice for others and world redemption through the shedding of blood—these and a hundred other symbols were utilized to take advantage of the religiously motivated individuals, while the awful struggle was painted as the Battle of Armageddon or the Holiest War of all the Ages. Thus were the Christian hosts mobilized for battle.[81]

Even in contemporary times we find a kindred sort of martial mythification. When surveying educational materials distributed by military chaplains, Berger and Pinard happened upon a compelling myth of the American fighting man:

Peace is a profession of conviction. The military man has a definite reason for what he does and for the uniform he wears. As an American he has learned so much about how to live he has tended to forget why he does so. He does not want to live for himself alone. He is granted life by a God who wants peace and understanding among men. His reason for living is, in essence, to advance that peace. Into whatever situation his military status takes him he goes in the spirit expressed by Air Force Captain Edwin G. Shank shortly before he was killed in Vietnam: "To do the best job possible for our country"—we would add, for our God.[82]

Conclusions: Those who suggest that to ritualize civil-religious discourse is to trivialize religion and patriotism and to render them impotent appear to have missed the sociological mark. Quite obviously for many people, God-and-country rallies are rhetorically attractive and psychologically rewarding experiences. On the other hand, Americans are not so foolish as to fail to notice the neutering of the discourse they hear at such gatherings, the opportunism displayed at times by civil pietists, the gushing emotionalism of the ceremonial events, or the querulous myths with which they as listeners are sometimes presented. In all of these things, however, Americans seem to take a delightfully pragmatic stance and to acknowledge such discourse for what it is—an amalgamation of poetic luxuriousness and cultural yearnings. All of this suggests that the willing suspension of disbelief is not a human function to be reserved exclusively for Broadway openings.

Prosaic Animus

Our inspection of the gods embodied in civil-religious rhetoric has indicated that—on the civil side at least—the esoteric continually loses out to the prosaic. Religio-political rhetoric is what might be called homocentric—it is constructed for and about mortal men. Indeed, Moberg would have us believe that such non-theocentricity is characteristic of all American religious discourse: "Worship for many people is partly or wholly homocentric. We worship God to serve human needs; we implore Deity to shape our own ends; we seek guidance in human affairs; we beseech God to give us peace and security amid the uncertainties of life; we seek immortality when life seems broken by death. In theory worship is theocentric; in practice it involves many homocentric goals and motivations."[83] Quite obviously, a national faith which found its roots in theocentric assumptions could not, as can the American civil religion, place its Godhead on the dollar bill or on a rainbow of bumper stickers. Recognizing its homocentricity, however, we can understand why proposed federal legislation has urged the cancelling of "In God We Trust" stamps with "Pray for Peace" designata.[84] And these prosaic impulses have been with us for some time. For example, Clark found starkly noncontemplative and secularized references to God in the nineteenth-century oratory of Bishop Matthew Simpson:

> He saw the hand of God in the invention of new ploughs, drilling machines, reapers, all designed to husband labor; he saw God in the building of the railroads so that the West was able in the hour of crisis to send its produce to the Eastern cities; he saw God in the simple matter of the sewing machine, in the discovery of the electric telegraph, in the starving of the poor in England at the time when they sympathized with the rebellion; he saw God in the sending of food by the North in "beautiful fulfillment of the Scriptures."[85]

It is understandable that we would find such refrains in a society long noted for its pragmatism. There appears never to have been a clearcut bifurcation between the sacred and the secular in American theology: "American religion is . . . non-theological and non-liturgical; it is . . . occupied with the things of the world to a degree that has become a byword among European churchmen," says Will Herberg.[86] If such is true of America's religions in general, it stands to reason that such would be true of *civil*-religious discourse in particular. Rather than finding metaphysical flights from the "Alone to the Alone" in such rhetoric,[87] we find it to be imbued with the most practical and prosaic of concerns:

> A contrivance called "God's Float" was rushed to completion [for a parade], but there was considerable embarrassment because of the shortage of appropriate materials. The float could not look Catholic, Protestant or Jewish—at least not *too* Catholic, Protestant or Jewish. It would have to be given some dignified place of honor in the parade. But where? Finally, it was put first, and at the heart of the display was placed a rather innocuous and not-quite-denominational building surrounded with mottoes reading "In God We Trust" and "Freedom of Worship."[88]

Sociologists might explain the practical (some would call it profane) flavor of our civil-religious discourse by looking to the capitalistic and ruggedly individualistic nature of the people who have sustained it. Scholars of religion might account for such suasory features by noting the non-contemplative roots supportive of American theology in the main. Historians would offer still other explanations. I would like to suggest that a rhetorical interpretation of such phenomena will serve us best, however. By accepting the notion that civil piety is largely a public affair and that cutting across it are strong but simple motivational vectors, we can better understand its rather sober manifestations.

Publicness

At least one way of explaining the prosaic nature of civil-religious discourse is to recognize that the bargain struck by church and state in America was a contract regulating and encouraging public (even mass) rhetorical statements. The civil-religious compact was one conceived by and for national religious and political leaders. Equally, it was a rhetoric designed originally to short-circuit national difficulties which could arise between church and state. It is more an historical curiosity than anything else that its themes have been appropriated by local congregations of the national religion. The suggestion being made here is that to misunderstand or to treat as insignificant the public nature of civil-religious discourse in America is to fail to appreciate its *raison d'etre*.

In supporting such a claim, we can turn to the distinguished historian, Winthrop Hudson, who declares: "'Civic religion,' the 'religion of the republic,' was *public* religion, a religion available to all through natural reason. 'Spiritual religion' was *private* religion, an 'experienced' religion that was intensely personal. The one was preoccupied with the nation and its mission; the other was preoccupied with individuals and their redemption."[89] The importance of Hudson's theoretical distinction is apparent. We can take his suggestion to mean that it is quite inappropriate to apply private criteria when assessing a rhetorical institution like American civil piety. That is, it might be quite legitimate for a believing Catholic to castigate the Jansenistic remarks made by a local pastor. However, were the parishioner to react with *equal* outrage at the pastor's participation in an Arbor Day ceremony, he or she would be confusing what should have been distinct (private and public) priorities.

In actuality, of course, most Americans make just the sort of distinctions we are suggesting here when evaluating the public and not-so-public rhetoric they hear daily. Most Americans hardly expect a confessional stance to be taken in the popular remarks of their elected officials. Most Americans assent to Gerald Ford's rhetorical priorities: "My faith is a very personal thing. It is not something one shouts from the housetop or wears on his sleeve. For me, my religious feeling is a deep personal faith I rely on for guidance from my God."[90] Most Americans, evidently, were unconcerned that Dwight Eisenhower's personal religious sentiments were out of sync with his presidential piety, as is reported by Billy Graham:

> When he become President, he brought a strong sense of dedication to his office. He introduced a prayer he wrote himself into his inaugural address and began the practice of devoting a minute of silent prayer at the beginning of cabinet meetings. Many of the cabinet meetings he had opened in prayer.
> He joined and regularly attended the National Presbyterian Church in Washington. *Before he became President, he was not a member of any church.* He called Dr. Ed Elson, the pastor of the church, and Dr. Elson gave him several hours of private Biblical instruction and

teaching. The President of the United States was baptized and made a public profession of his faith in Jesus Christ. He became one of the most dedicated churchmen in the nation.

I talked to him many times about this experience, and *I am convinced that he made his personal commitment to Christ as a boy; but he made it publicly after he had become President of the United States.*[91] (Emphasis added.)

Dwight Eisenhower knew, as we know, that a public rhetoric like civil-religious discourse must concern itself with the sundry philosophical predilections of its hearers, seeking the most common of rhetorical denominators, if it is to be effective. The civil pietist must sacrifice the delicate individuality of a particular theological and/or political system for one which will motivate equally the members of a bewilderingly diverse audience. Thus voided of sectarian and partisan arguments, civil-religious rhetoric often takes on the ritualistic, non-existential, and expediently complex nature we have been describing in this chapter.

Presidents (and archbishops), then, must be vigilant about their private and public personae. In this connection, Richard Nixon's White House tapes did the unthinkable—they permitted his private morality to be displayed under the klieg lights of national scrutiny. His civil-religious heresy was not so much that he crossed the indistinct line of ethical principle but that he was not publicly circumspect. As adherents of the civil religion, Americans can forgive many things in their national leaders, but public gaucheness is not one of them. As adherents to private ethical systems, of course, they render other (usually, more denunciatory) judgments of Mr. Nixon's Watergate behavior as well.

Emotional Hardiness

The prosaic cast of much civil-religious rhetoric derives as much from its use as a helpmate to the American people during times of crisis as it does from its public gestation and rationale. Religio-political rhetoric acts as a prime agent of disaster relief and has always acted thusly:

In the presence of a storm or a cannonade at sea or in the exigencies of combat in the field, and notably in the great exigencies of national destiny such as a presidential assassination, the extraordinary range of American denominational religiosity is pretty much contracted into the essentials for men in peril, wherever and whatever their religion.[92]

That is not to say, as we have seen, that civil-religious rhetoric administers tangible palliatives. Rather, such rhetoric is used to encourage its audience to view the crisis at hand as but a momentary tribulation for a nation whose grandeur has long been assured:

> America became great, not because of any material wealth, but because of the spiritual fiber of our forebearers regardless of creed. In every crisis and emergency in our Nation's history, Americans, from the leaders on down, have called on God to aid, comfort and guide them, and their pleas have always been answered. SO MAY IT EVER BE![93]

As Herbert Schneider reports, Wilson and Roosevelt often resorted to civil-religious themes during wartime. According to Schneider, these rhetorical choices served to give "a general religious solemnity to the struggles and to suggest officially that 'in God we trust.'"[94] In addition to mythifying the particular conflagration at hand, such rhetoric illustrates the "primordial impulse to invoke the symbols of social unity" during times of conflict.[95] Thus exalted and befriended, the American people can then make supernatural sense out of their uncomfortable empirical realities—or so goes the rhetorical hypothesis of militant civil piety. Understanding the "crisis function" of religio-political rhetoric may help us to appreciate why so many unofficial civil religionists (like Billy James Hargis and Fred Schwarz) have co-opted the themes of civil piety when combating, for example, the Communist menace.

Optimism: A truly distinctive feature of civil-religious discourse is its zealous and enthusiastic spirit. The American civil religion has never been popular among Sartrian doomsdayers; rather, according to such rhetoric, the American people can attain most anything.

Will Herberg credits the simple optimism of American civil piety to the idealism found within the Judaeo-Christian traditions from which it sprang and by which it is nourished.[96] The rhetorical explanation for such themes is a bit less complicated: any public rhetoric which purports to unify and to motivate a heterogeneous population and to insure that church and state continue to be amiable partners in the national enterprise could hardly be otherwise. "The true and operative religion of America is not that of the churches at all, with their pessimistic general confessions," argued Willard Sperry in 1946, "but that of the state with its declarations of independence."[97]

Sperry's thesis is attractive in the 1970s as well. After all, the market on optimism has not been cornered by election-year politicians alone. A generous share belongs equally to establishment preachers and to politicized churchmen like Ezra Taft Benson. Note in the following passage (from a speech Benson gave on December 4, 1973, to the students of Brigham Young University) that no manner of hardship can prevent a Holy Nation from triumphing:

> Yes, we have a rich heritage, but may I remind you that nations ofttimes sow the seeds of their own destruction even while enjoying unprecedented prosperity, even before reaching the zenith or the peak of their power. I think history clearly indicates that this is often the case. When it appears that all is well, ofttimes the very seeds of destruction are sown, sometimes unwittingly. Most of the great civilizations of the world have not been conquered from without until they have destroyed themselves from within by sowing these seeds of destruction.[98]

But,

> Every true Latter-day Saint should love the United States of America— the most generous nation under heaven—the Lord's base of operations in these last days. May we do all in our power to strengthen and safeguard this base and increase our freedom. This nation will, I feel sure, endure. It is God-ordained for a glorious purpose.[99]

Civil-religious rhetoric, it would appear, typically ends on the upbeat.

Emotional Simplicity: "The Pilgrim Fathers," intoned Norman Vincent Peale, set forth in "little ships across a stormy sea, driven not by the winds that raged the Atlantic and caught the sails of their little boats, but by the mighty conviction that as sons of God nobody could make slaves of them."[100] Cynics, of course, could argue that such emotional simplicity is typical of Peale's unique faith in hope. This does not appear to be the case, however. While civil-religious discourse is often more sophisticated than Peale's, civil piety is normally uncomplicated inventionally. It relies on relatively straightforward commonplaces, hitting hard at the listener's most basic motivations. That is, civil-religious rhetoric depends for its effect on the audience's adherence to certain simple, archetypal themes—God meets nation, God loves nation, God sustains nation—and seeks only to create telling (if necessary, local) variations on such themes. "The religion of Washington politicians stops with this simple identification of goodness and faith," writes popularist Paul Blanshard, "controversial theology is completely taboo"[101] in civil piety.

To understand why such rhetorical dictates are followed carefully by politicians, we need only to be reminded of the public, ritualistic exigences which typically call forth civil piety. The stock themes of "justice and magnanimity, humanity and valor, the virtues of the heart before the head, a simple trust in God"[102] and so forth are found in civil-religious rhetoric for the precise reasons that they are found (oftentimes in complex forms) in many forms of public communication, not to mention in popular entertainment. Such themes are compelling to us collectively, no matter how vapid they may appear to us as individuals in private.

While scholars and theologians may denounce these themes as just so much emotional sop for an ignorant audience, it must be remembered that the richer, albeit divisive, themes of sectarian religion and partisan politics wait in the wings . . . beckoning unbecomingly. Unless we wish to throw down the rather workable contractual edifice described in this essay, civil piety will have to do. By accepting the emotional simplicity of our civil pietists—as well as the many other features of their rhetoric we have observed in this chapter—we are accepting what is for many a valued public heritage. By viewing civil-religious discourse from a rhetorical point of view and not from the vantage point of the theologian or the cultural critic, we may keep it in its proper perspective, taking it just as seriously as good sense and social realities warrant.

Conclusion

When concluding his seminal essay on civil religion, Robert Bellah urged that the ethnocentricity of American civil religion be substituted in our national life for a far-reaching and catholic, indeed, international, self-knowledge. Said Bellah:

So far the flickering flame of the United Nations burns too low to be the focus of a cult, but the emergence of a genuine trans-national sovereignty would certainly change this. It would necessitate the incorporation of vital international symbolism into our civil religion, or, perhaps a better way of putting it, it would result in American civil religion becoming simply one part of a new civil religion of the world. It is useless to speculate on the form such a civil religion might take, though it obviously would draw on religious traditions beyond the sphere of Biblical religion alone. Fortunately, since the American civil religion is not the worship of the American nation but an understanding of the American experience in the light of ultimate and universal reality, the reorganization entailed by such a new situation need not disrupt the American civil religion's continuity. A world civil religion could be accepted as a fulfillment and not a denial of American civil religion. Indeed, such an outcome has been the eschatological hope of American civil religion from the beginning. To deny such an outcome would be to deny the meaning of America itself.[103]

Attractive though Bellah's goal-state may be, the realities of cross-cultural understanding and, more important, of misunderstanding, threaten to confound Bellah's experiment in civil-religious internationalism at its very inception. For if we have described *American* civil-religious rhetoric accurately in this chapter, could we expect its international relative to be fundamentally different? Could the admonitions of an international deity be any more exacting than those issued by America's own twenty-eight-flavored God? Could the United Nations devise a civil-religious contract replete with universally attractive, activist, and existentially bent codicils? Could a satisfactory rhetorical formula for describing our international destiny be anything but expedient and complex when mouthed simultaneously by a Rabin and a Sadat? If an American Catholic and a Protestant fundamentalist can brook one another only under the occasional canopy of public ritual, can we expect anything more from an interaction between a destitute Buddhist and a well-fed German Lutheran? And finally, could any public profession of an international civil religion be envisioned without our also anticipating the optimistic emotionality we have observed in its domestic counterpart? Obviously, these are all highly rhetorical questions about an unquestionably rhetorical matter. Thus, while our globe may well be becoming an increasingly compact village, it seems unlikely that anything as abstract and pre-articulate as a "civil religion" can, alone, assuage the very real problems associated with such profoundly complex forms of international shrinkage.

Throughout this essay, however, it has never been my intention to quibble with Bellah's philosophical yearnings. Surely it is wise for the American people to reckon with the press of international responsibility, with the mistreatment of minority groups, and with the philosophical emptiness native to so much of the religiously tinged political discourse we hear daily. But to subscribe to Bellah's ideals is not to condone his several reifications of politico-rhetorical life in the United States. While it may make for adequate shirt-sleeved philosophy to speak of the existence of *an* American civil religion, it makes little empirical sense for Bellah to deny constantly the cultural pluralism which foreswears all such premature symbolic homogenizing. Nevertheless, Bellah persists:

> No one has changed a great nation without appealing to *its* soul, without stimulating *a* national idealism, as even those who have called themselves materialists have discovered. Culture is *the* key to revolution, religion is *the* key to culture. If *we* win the political struggle, *we* will not even know what *we* want unless *we* have *a* new vision of man, *a* new sense of human possibility, and *a* new conception of the ordering of liberty, the constitution of freedom.[104] (Emphasis added.)

Noble sentiments all. But implicit in Bellah's eschaton is a type of ideological imperialism, a demand for a set of public symbols which will suffice for all Americans. More than likely, the American people will have none of this. Oh, yes, they will allow their preachers and politicians to talk about *the* national consensus, about *the* American ideal, and about *the* God-beholdin' American people; *but they will not easily forget, it seems to me, that all of this is talk.* Because it is talk, the American people can revel in it, carp at it, demand new versions of it, glorify it, dismiss it. But should some far-sighted prelate or politician fail to notice the fine print imbedded in the civil-religious contract and to misperceive its rhetorical nature, the American people will come a-marching.

As a people, we seem to take delight in the religiosity of our country only to the extent that such a notion remains safely ensconced in the realm of symbolic reality. And so, let both clergyman and congressman be warned—civic piety, not civil religion, is the order of this and every day in these tenuously united states of ours. No matter how anachronistic some may find his politics to be, no matter what variety of reductionism others may detect in his theology, and no matter how vague the existential implications of his remarks may appear to some, Billy Graham's brand of civic piety is probably as much a harbinger of the rhetorical future as it is an echo of the American experience:

> This is all a part of the American heritage—a nation that believes in God, a nation that flies the Christian flag, a nation that believes in the providences of God in her national life.
>
> Who of us can forget the picture of George Washington in prayer at Valley Forge, and then his taking his small army and routing the British, thus bringing about our victory in the war of the Revolution? Who can forget the words of Benjamin Franklin as he called the Constitutional Convention to prayer and out of that prayer meeting came the Constitution of the United States? Who can forget Abraham Lincoln and his cabinet on their knees many times during the Civil War, not praying for victory, but asking that God's will be done? Who can forget the great epochs in American life in which we have honored God and recognized God? I say that it is the secret of America's prosperity, America's strength, and this is the hope of America's future.[105]

POSTLUDE

In this essay, my central contention has been that to deny the significance of the rhetorical dimension of American civic piety is to misperceive its very essence. Like many things human, and like most things American, civic piety does not simply "exist." It exists because the American people and their leaders have rather conscientiously determined to wage their struggles of church and state on rhetorical battlegrounds, realizing that the casualties of rhetorical war always live to speak another day. They have realized, too, that public rhetoric is an incredibly potent vehicle through which the "social symbiosis"[1] of religion and government can be effected, maintained, and made palatable.

In this essay, we have observed a commonplace and important feature of life in the United States. We have witnessed the panorama of civic piety in America, a spectrum of discourse which is both variegated and possessed of subtle hues. We have seen that to view rhetorically enlivened civic piety as religion-like may well be to distort its essence as a symbolic and very human creation. And we have noted that a "contractual" view of civil-religious-rhetorical bonds appears to offer significant heuristic insight into the ways in which Americans choose to live their public lives.

More recently in this essay, I have attempted to point up four rather specific properties of civic piety: its expedient complexity, its non-existential content, its ritualistic presence, and its prosaic animus. Many observers, of course, might well view such features as bespeaking the most unfortunate aspects of the civil-religious compact. One California clergyman, for example, has likened civic piety to "spiritual aspirin," since "it doesn't cost much, doesn't do much, and isn't worth much."[2] Such an interpretation, I would submit, constitutes much too frontal a criticism. Our cleric is right, of course, in suggesting that American civic piety doesn't cost much. Except in the eyes of the most staunch denominationalists and separationists, little of significance seems to be lost when one of our chief executives requests the help of a God in whom he may have little personal confidence. Also, the participation of religious leaders in our Orange Bowls requires many Americans to expend only a small measure of grace and good sense as they bow their heads while waiting for the kickoff. When the ubiquity of civic piety is contrasted with the tortuous twists and turns of American political fortunes and the religious revolutions and counter-revolutions which have beset the American theological establishment throughout its history, it seems that a political benediction or two is a small price to pay for providing some semblance of collective harmony and national destiny for those who need them.

To suggest that civic piety doesn't "do much" (or isn't "worth much") is, as we have seen, both right and wrong. Because civic piety is normally devoid of existential punch—finding instead its *raison d'etre* in the worlds of myth and symbol—its tangible accomplishments are, in one sense, hard to discern. As has been suggested throughout this essay, however, the American people have had no experience with a national life unattended by a surrogate church-state. Whereas the legal principle of disestablishment is the mortar which has kept the wall of separation in tact throughout our nation's history, it is our civil-pietists-turned-artisans who have kept that partition refurbished, decorative, and patently functional. Although the American people may well have transmuted Jefferson's wall of separation into a semi-permeable membrane through which civil-religious messages flow generously, it is a significant fact that the edifice has withstood the tests of time and partisanship. And while Richard Fenn is undoubtedly right when arguing that civil-religious discourse has not (especially in recent times) served to perform a truly integrative function for American society,[3] national civic piety has managed to keep in check all would-be rival "integrators," forcing the latter to vend their divisive wares in more local contexts.

Recently, however, a number of commentators have

suggested that the death knell of civic piety is being sounded, and that church and state will soon abrogate the rhetorical contract they have signed and constantly renewed. Typically, three strains of argument have been offered to support such a claim: religious, political, and sociological. Some observers feel, for example, that because American Catholics have been frustrated in their attempts to receive public aid for their private schools, they soon will truculantly refuse to participate in our civil-religious ceremonies. In addition, fundamentalist Protestants bemoan prayerless public schools, Jews have never been regarded as swimming in the civil-religious mainstream, and, as Cherry has indicated,[4] atheists and agnostics too have a right to expect participation in any *civil* religion that calls itself American.

American civic piety soon may have battles to wage on political and sociological fronts as well. For example, the Vietnam War was the first major American conflagration whose holy purpose could not be easily discovered by many American clergymen. Too, our unofficial civil religionists—the Carl McKintires, the Billy James Hargises, and the Fred Schwartzes—are becoming more insistent that the accomodationistic rhetoric of mainstream civic piety be curtailed and that America once again assume a straightforward, messianic role in the world. Finally, as we have seen earlier in this essay, the separationists are continually warning us that American civic piety calls into question this nation's historical distaste for even pseudo-theocratic governmental structures.

These are all serious charges. Yet, like so many of the comments which have been made about the American civil religion, these fatalistic remarks credit civic piety with more transcendent importance than seems sensible. If the last two hundred years have taught us anything, it is that the American people—as a people—can tolerate, even relish, legion cultural anomalies. No matter how vociferous contemporary Catholics, Protestants, Jews, antiwar activists, Communist baiters, and separationists may become, such a cadre is perhaps no more fundamentally diverse in cultural or philosophical predilection than was the "movement which began with the first settlers at Jamestown," as Ernest Bates pointed out more than thirty years ago:

> The American faith . . . was a complex, an amalgamation, of hundreds of warring faiths. It could not possibly be closely knit or approach a logical unity such as we find in medieval Catholicism or in

modern fascism or communism. Tolerance of diversity was one of its essential characteristics. At its basis was a kind of residuum of common qualities found in nearly all of its constituent movements. Above that were elements, adopted now from one group, now from another, because they proved to possess, for one or another reason, survival value. It was bound to be shot through with logical contradictions. Such unity as it possessed, over and above a certain basic identity of spirit, was largely a union of opposites. Its method was compromise, its result assimilation. It was not "thinly dieted on dew," but lived like an organism through the neutralization of poisons.[5]

The conditions which Bates specifies as giving rise to American civic piety seem to hold today as well. Bicentennial America is neither more nor less beset by cultural, religious, and political incongruities than was its counterpart in Jamestown. Unless the American people suddenly choose *not* to accomodate one another through public ritual, or to recreate and promulgate their national myths, or to continue to honor the rhetorically based contract they have enforced upon church and state, civic piety—of a changing yet changeless variety—will continue to distinguish the cultural and symbolic landscape of the United States.

NOTES

Prelude

1. "Civil Religion in America," *Daedalus* (Winter 1967): 1-21.

2. Burke's commentaries on symbolic action interpenetrate all of his works. For a particularly good introduction to his perspective, see *Language as Symbolic Action: Essays on Life, Literature, and Method.*

3. "The Carrot and Stick as Handmaidens of Persuasion in Conflict Situations," in *Perspectives on Communication in Social Conflict,* ed. Gerald R. Miller and Herbert W. Simons (Englewood Cliffs, N.J.: Prentice-Hall, 1974), p. 188.

4. "Genres in an Emerging Tradition: An Anthropological Approach to Religious Communication," in *Changing Perspectives in the Scientific Study of Religion,* ed. Allen W. Eister (New York: Wiley, 1974), p. 252.

5. "The Civil Religion of Ethnic Americans: The Viewpoint of a Catholic Sociologist," *Religious Education* (September-October 1975): 500

6. Personal communication, January 1976. Gregg is professor of speech communication at the Pennsylvania State University, University Park, Pa.

7. The reader who is interested in a contemporary survey of the rhetorical viewpoint would be well advised to consult: Carroll C. Arnold, *The Criticism of Oral Rhetoric* (Columbus, Ohio: Charles Merrill, 1974); Lloyd Bitzer and Edwin Black, eds., *The Prospect of Rhetoric* (Englewood Cliffs, N.J.: Prentice-Hall, 1971); Douglas Ehninger, ed., *Contemporary Rhetoric* (Glenview, Ill.: Scott-Foresman, 1972); and Robert L. Scott and Bernard L. Brock, eds., *Methods of Rhetorical Criticism: A Twentieth Century Perspective* (New York: Harper, 1972).

Those readers interested in sampling sustained rhetorical inquiries should see: Wayne Booth, *The Rhetoric of Fiction* (Chicago: University of Chicago Press, 1961); Kenneth Burke, *A Rhetoric of Motives* (Berkeley: University of California Press, 1969); Raymond F. Howes, ed., *Historical Studies of Rhetoric and Rhetoricians* (Ithaca, N.Y.: Cornell University

Press, 1961); George Kennedy, *The Art of Persuasion in Greece* (Princeton, N.J.: Princeton University Press, 1963); G. P. Mohrmann, Charles J. Stewart, and Donovan J. Ochs, eds., *Explorations in Rhetorical Criticism* (University Park: Pennsylvania State University Press, 1973); C. Perelman and L. Olbrechts-Tyteca, *The New Rhetoric* (South Bend, Ind.: University of Notre Dame Press, 1969); and Karl Wallace, *Understanding Discourse* (Baton Rouge: Louisiana State University Press, 1970).

8. *New York Times,* 23 December 1952.
9. See Paul Blanshard, *God and Man in Washington,* p. 3.
10. Joseph F. Costanzo, *This Nation Under God,* pp. 36-37.
11. Quoted in William L. Miller, *Piety Along the Potomac,* p. 42.

Chapter

1. Michael Novak, *Choosing Our King,* p. 303 ff.
2. Conrad Cherry, "American Sacred Ceremonies," in *American Mosaic: Social Patterns of Religion in the United States,* ed. Phillip E. Hammond and Benton Johnson (New York: Random House, 1970), p. 304.
3. George N. Gordon, *Persuasion: The Theory and Practice of Manipulative Communication,* p. 198.
4. Novak, *Choosing,* p. 127.
5. Robert S. Alley, *So Help Me God,* pp. 78-79.
6. Will Herberg, "Religion in a Secularized Society: The New Shape of Religion in America," in *The Sociology of Religion: An Anthology,* ed. Richard D. Knudten (New York: Meredith, 1967), p. 475.
7. Quoted in Alley, p. 120.
8. David W. Glockley, executive vice president, Religion in American Life, personal communication, 1 March 1974.
9. *God is Alive (and Working on Madison Avenue)* (pamphlet issued by Religion in American Life, n.d.), not paginated.
10. Quoted in Mary H. Weinberg, "The Flag Lady," *Indianapolis Star Magazine,* 6 February 1972, p. 11.
11. Herbert Schneider, *Religion in Twentieth Century America,* p. 58. With regard to the religious-military establishment, Schneider's remarks are especially apt. Harvey Cox, for example, has recounted for us the pervasive influence enjoyed by organized religion in the nation's military units: "Here are some statistics, however, supplied by the Defense Department, which give some indication of the number of persons involved: In July 1970 the Defense Department reported there were a total of 4,020 chaplains serving in the Army (1,792), Navy (1,068) and Air Force (1,160). The chaplain's average age is about 40 (a little younger in the Army, a little older in the Air Force). In the Army, 1,040 are Protestants, 600 are Catholics, 60 are Jews and 5 are Eastern Orthodox. The ratios among denominations are about the same in the other branches. It is interesting to note in glancing at the list of Protestant denominations represented,

that although the 'mainline' denominations understandably supply most chaplains, there are also chaplains from the Christian Missionary Alliance Church (6), Church of the Nazarene (31), Churches of God in North America (2), Free Will Baptists (2), Moravians (4), and the Salvation Army (3). The Defense Department lists no chaplains from the Society of Friends, Buddhists, International Society for Krishna Consciousness ('Hare Krishnas'), Amish, or Black Muslims. Over 80 percent of the chaplains are career officers as opposed to men serving only a limited term." *Military Chaplains: From a Religious Military to a Military Religion*, ed. Harvey G. Cox (New York: American Report Press, 1971), p. xii.

12. Harry P. Kerr, "Politics and Religion in Colonial Fast and Thanksgiving Sermons, 1763-1783," *Quarterly Journal of Speech* 46, no. 4 (December 1960): 382.

13. Howard H. Martin, "The Fourth of July Oration," *Quarterly Journal of Speech* 44, no. 4 (December 1958): 394.

14. William Gribbin, *The Churches Militant*, p. 19.

15. Will Herberg, *Protestant, Catholic and Jew*, p. 65. Alley, p. 91, reveals the civil-religious tones of the fifties most dramatically when he reports: "The White House religion, which so encouraged the nation in its piety and aided in the rise to prominence of Billy Graham as a political force, placed little emphasis on sect or faith commitment, only on a kind of divine feeling. It was the era of the 'Man Upstairs' and prayer before college football games. The people felt quite self-righteous, though the fear of Communism and the 'bomb' pervaded the fifties and Sputnik frightened the nation in 1957. For many, prayer was a substitute for thinking about problems. It was during the reign of Ike that the country came closer than ever before to establishing a civil religion. It would have been modified Puritanism divested of ethical and theological content. There was a totally uncritical approach to the Bible, a fact which is attested by the various motion pictures of the period. Modern biblical scholarship was rejected or ignored. It was a decade of simplistic faith when Hollywood could market 'Peter Marshall' and audiences would respond with tears and faith. It was a nostalgic effort to return to the old-time religion."

16. Leo Pfeffer, *Church, State, and Freedom*, p. 192.

17. David L. Cohn, "Politics in a God-Fearin' Key," *Saturday Review*, 3 April 1954, p. 12.

18. "The Child's Political World," *Midwest Journal of Political Science* 6 (August 1962): 238-39.

19. Willmoore Kendall and George W. Carey, *The Basic Symbols of the American Political Tradition*.

20. See Kenneth Burke, *Attitudes Toward History*, vol. 1.

21. Gordon, *Persuasion*, p. 194.

22. *Time*, 19 November 1973, p. 18.

23. Quoted in Norman Vincent Peale, *A New Birth of Freedom* (New York: Foundation for Christian Living, n.d.), p. 10.

24. *Newsweek*, 24 June 1974, p. 33.

25. Novak, *Choosing*, p. 302.

26. Quoted in *Indianapolis Star*, 30 January 1972.

27. (Van Nuys, Calif.: Bible Voice, Inc., 1970), p. 30. Robert Jewett, in a brilliant book entitled *The Captain America Complex*, refers to what he calls "hot zeal" and "cool zeal." The heat given off by unofficial civil religionists in their rhetoric contrasts sharply, as we shall see, with the ice-cold, "distancing" rhetoric employed by their official counterparts.

28. Reprinted in Boone et al.

29. Martin E. Marty, "Sects and Cults." *The Annals of the American Academy of Political and Social Science*, vol. 332, p. 128.

30. Lloyd F. Bitzer, "The Rhetorical Situation," *Philosophy and Rhetoric*, vol. 1, no. 1, pp. 1-14.

31. Perhaps no better coverage of the wide scope of church-state interaction exists than that provided by Leo Pfeffer, *Church, State, and Freedom*.

32. Marty, "Sects and Cults," p. 129.

33. *The Christian Patriot* 30, no. 1 (January 1974): 6.

34. "Editorial: Senator Harold Hughes," *The N.A.C.P.A. Politikon* 3 (February 1974): 2.

35. Robert N. Bellah, "Civil Religion in America," *Daedalus* (Winter 1967), p. 14.

36. Quoted in Duncan Howlett, "The Sleeper in the Prayer Amendment," Address delivered at the All Souls Unitarian Church, Washington, D.C., 24 May 1964. While Billington's remarks are admittedly singular, a penchant for active and practical involvement with the vicissitudes of this world does indeed earmark the rhetoric of the civil-religious Right. As John Birch leader Tom Anderson has implied, to cling exclusively to symbolic influence is to forsake one's commitment to God and country: "What irritates *me* is seeing Christians used to destroy their own faith and the faith of this once-Christian nation. All that is necessary to cause fifty million American Christians—real Christians—to be murdered by the Communists is for Christian Americans to devote themselves exclusively to prayer and let the Communists take over our country!" See "For Christians: Put on the Whole armor of God," *American Opinion*, November 1972, p. 6.

37. *Christian Crusade Weekly*, 30 June 1974, p. 1.

38. *What is the Church League of America?* (Wheaton, Ill.: Church League of America, n.d.), p. 3.

39. Frank Hughes, *The Church League of America Story* (pamphlet issued by the Church League of America, n.d.).

40. *Christian Crusade Weekly*, 14 April 1974, p. 4.

41. Peter L. Berger and Daniel Pinard. "Military Religion: An Analysis of Educational Materials Disseminated by Chaplains," in *Military Chaplains*, p. 91.

42. Sidney E. Mead, *The Lively Experiment*, p. 152.

43. Kenneth L. Sheek, "Letter to the Editor," *Indianapolis Star*, 23 December 1973.

44. Smith is, in my terminology, a decidedly unofficial civil religionist and editor of a journal (*The Cross and the Flag*) which "makes its way through the mails in a plain brown wrapper." See Barnett Baskerville, "The Cross and the Flag: Evangelists of the Far Right," in *The Rhetoric of Our Times*, ed. J. Jeffery Auer (New York: Meredith, 1969), p. 434.

Chapter

1. Sherwood Eddy, *The Kingdom of God and the American Dream*, p. 79.
2. Charles Smith, *Why Read the Bible in the Public Schools?* (New York: National Liberal League, Inc., 1949), not paginated.
3. "The Case for Separation," in *Religion in America*, ed. John Cogley (New York: Meridian, 1958), p. 59.
4. "Commentary," in *The Religious Situation: 1968*, ed. Donald R. Cutler (Boston: Beacon Press, 1968), p. 358. See also Andrew M. Greeley, *Unsecular Man*, p. 129.
5. For a more complete discussion of such matters, see Leo Pfeffer, *Church, State, and Freedom*, p. 108.
6. Ernest S. Bates, *American Faith*, pp. 83-84.
7. Don Higginbotham, "The Relevance of the American Revolution," *Anglican Theological Review*, no. 1 (July 1973): 29.
8. Edwin Gaustad, *A Religious History of America*, p. 257.
9. Loren Beth, *The American Theory of Church and State*, p. 72.
10. Bernard Bailyn, *The Ideological Origins of the American Revolution*, p. 271.
11. See Annemarie de Waal Malefijt, *Religion and Culture*, p. 235.
12. Billy Graham, "White House Sermon, March 15, 1970," in *White House Sermons*, ed. Ben Hibbs (New York: Harper and Row. Inc., 1972), p. 136. Anthropologist of religion, Annemarie de Waal Malefijt, remarks: "Diviners often wield a significant amount of political power. . . . The rules of augury were secret, and the signs were usually vague enough to allow alternate interpretations in order to please the rulers in power and to dispose of others." (See her *Religion and Culture*, p. 217). When Richard Nixon was the Grand Shaman of the American civil religion, at least, Billy Graham's divinations were found to be particularly valuable.
13. Conrad Cherry, *God's New Israel*, p. 13.
14. Peter Berger, *The Sacred Canopy*, p. 58.
15. Michael C. Thomas and Charles C. Flippen, "American Civil Religion: An Empirical Study," *Social Forces* 51 (December 1972): 218-25.
16. Robert N. Bellah, "American Civil Religion in the 1970's," *Anglican Theological Review*, no. 1 (July 1973): 8.
17. John F. Wilson, "The Status of 'Civil Religion' in America," in *The Religion of the Republic*, ed. Elwyn A. Smith (Philadelphia: Fortress Press, 1971), p. 15.
18. Ibid., p. 14.
19. Bellah, "Civil Religion in 1970's," p. 9. Robert Stauffer also feels that rigorous use of the term *religion* in this context is unnecessarily constraining. See his "Civil Religion, Technocracy, and the Private Sphere: Further

Comments on Cultural Integration in Advanced Societies," *Journal for the Scientific Study of Religion* 12, no. 4 (December 1973): 417.

20. O'Dea delineates each of these functions more precisely in *Sociology and the Study of Religion*, pp. 205-207, 262-67.

21. Robert S. Alley, *So Help Me God*, p. 18.

22. O'Dea, pp. 240-55.

23. Alternative explanations for the American civil religion's having escaped O'Dea's problems would be that it is too "young" to have been institutionalized or that it has been hardy enough to foresee and to take steps to prevent such vicissitudes from arising. The first alternative seems unlikely when we consider that the "religion" has existed for almost two hundred years (according to Bellah), a time-span which is more than sufficient for producing the natural developmental problems O'Dea sees as common to most all religions. Also, the fact that the "hierarchy" of our national faith, as well as the attitudes and motivations of its "members," have changed so fundamentally and so rapidly since 1776 seems to indicate that scant attention could have been directed to heading off such naturally occurring difficulties.

24. Wilson, "Status of 'Civil Religion,'" pp. 20-21.

25. Robert N. Bellah, "Civil Religion in America," *Daedalus* (Winter 1967), p. 1.

26. Dwight D. Eisenhower, "First Inaugural Address, January 20, 1953," in *Inaugural Addresses of the Presidents of the United States* (Washington, D.C.: U.S. Government Printing Office, 1969), p. 256.

27. Bellah, "Civil Religion in 1970's," p. 19.

28. See, for example, Charles Henderson, *The Nixon Theology*.

29. "Feature Review," *Religious Education* (September-October 1975), p. 552.

30. "Two Kinds of Two Kinds of Civil Religion," in *American Civil Religion*, ed. Russell E. Richey and Donald G. Jones (New York: Harper, 1974), p. 141.

31. In Richey and Jones, p. 137.

32. Ibid., p. 135.

33. Alley, p. 17.

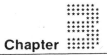

Chapter

1. Peter Berger, *The Noise of Solemn Assemblies*, p. 60.

2. "The Present Embarrassment of the Church," in *Religion in America*, ed. John Cogley (New York: Meridian, 1958), p. 23.

3. Benjamin Weiss, *God in American History*, p. 36.

4. Reprinted in Weiss, pp. 37-38.

5. Weiss, p. 36.

6. Berger, *The Sacred Canopy*, p. 33.

7. Madlyn Murray O'Hair, *Freedom Under Siege*.

8. "The King's Chapel and the King's Court," *Christianity and Crisis,* 4 August 1969, p. 211.

9. "Civil Religion in America," *Daedalus* (Winter 1967): 3.

10. Leo Pfeffer, *Church, State, and Freedom,* p. 109.

11. Ibid.

12. Sidney Mead, *The Lively Experiment,* p. 65.

13. Quoted in Paul Blanshard, *God and Man in Washington,* p. 100.

14. Ibid.

15. Ibid.

16. Mead, p. 97.

17. For more information on such matters, see Mead.

18. See William Gribbin, *The Churches Militant.*

19. Ray Abrams, *Preachers Present Arms,* p. 121.

20. Mead, p. 65.

21. Blanshard, p. 25.

22. Frederick Fox, "The National Day of Prayer," *Theology Today* 26, no. 3 (October 1972): 273.

23. Franklin Littell, *From State Church to Pluralism,* pp. xi-xii.

24. O'Hair, pp. 3-5.

25. Oswald C. J. Hoffmann, "Faith and Force," *And Our Defense is Sure,* ed. H. D. Moore, E. A. Ham, and C. E. Hobgood (New York: Abingdon, 1964), p. 77.

26. Bernard Bell, *Crowd Culture,* p. 98.

27. Alan Heimert, *Religion and the American Mind,* pp. 540-41.

28. Berger, *Solemn Assemblies,* p. 67. During times of conflict, members of the clergy have often leapt to the defense of the American nation. Harry Kerr reports that during the Revolution, for example, the election sermons played an important role in preparing the way for the Revolution and for the establishment of a democratic form of government in America. Also, in World War I, Roman Catholic prelate John Cardinal Farley reminded his congregation that "As Catholics we owe unswerving allegiance to the government of America, and it is our sacred duty to answer with alacrity every demand our country makes upon our loyalty and devotion." At approximately the same time, the pastor of the First Baptist Church of New London, Connecticut, "preached in his [chaplain's] uniform with a machine gun and an American flag on the platform beside him." In more recent times, the American clergy was asked by a federal agency to be ready to launch the "spiritual mobilization of the country in case of war," while, at the same time, the agency was inquiring into the possibility of using church buildings as civil defense shelters! Besides rendering rhetorical assistance to the government when requested, it would seem that organized religion is required to share with its "partner" many of its non-rhetorical possessions as well. See Harry P. Kerr, "The Election Sermon: Primer for Revolutionaries," *Speech Monographs* 29, no. 1 (March 1962): p. 18; Abrams, pp. 73 and 245-46; and Berger, *Solemn Assemblies,* p. 61.

29. Will Herberg, *Protestant, Catholic and Jew,* p. 286.

30. Ibid., p. 96.

31. Loren Beth, *The American Theory of Church and State*, p. 151.

32. For a fuller discussion, see ibid., p. 124 ff.

33. *Time*, 17 December 1973, p. 78.

34. Quoted in ibid.

35. Harry P. Kerr, "Politics and Religion in Colonial Fast and Thanksgiving Sermons, 1763-1783," *Quarterly Journal of Speech* 46, no. 4 (December 1960): 376.

36. Heimert, p. 240.

37. For a more detailed discussion of such issues, see Abrams, p. 207.

38. Quoted in Fay Valentine, *Citizenship for Christians* (Nashville, Tenn.: Broadman Press, 1965), p. 17.

39. Nick Thimmesch, "The Lord and Harold Hughes," *Saturday Evening Post*, June-July 1974, p. 45.

40. Richard J. Neuhaus, "The War, the Churches, and Civil Religion," *The Annals* 387 (January 1970): 134.

41. Ibid.

42. Robert S. Alley, *So Help Me God*, p. 95.

43. Neuhaus, p. 130.

44. See ibid. p. 131.

45. Littell, p. 163.

Chapter

1. Kathleen Jamieson, "Generic Calcification: An Undiagnosed Rhetorical Malady," Paper presented at the annual convention of the Speech Communication Association, New York City, December 1974.

2. Kathleen Jamieson, "Generic Constraints and the Rhetorical Situation," *Philosophy and Rhetoric* 6, no. 3 (Summer 1973): 163.

3. Frederick Fox, "The National Day of Prayer," *Theology Today* 26, no. 3 (October 1972): 269.

4. Gabriel Fackre, "Of Hope and Judgment," in *Bicentennial Broadside* (New York: United Church Board for Homeland Ministries, 1975), p. 6.

5. "In God We Trust," *Christian Century*, 27 May 1964, p. 719.

6. Robert Alley, *So Help Me God*, p. 15.

7. Ibid.

8. Robert Bellah, "Civil Religion in America," *Daedalus* (Winter 1967), p. 7.

9. *Inaugural Addresses of the Presidents of the United States* (Washington, D.C.: U.S. Government Printing Office, 1969). All subsequent quotations from the presidential inaugurals have been extracted from this source.

10. A careful inspection of Richard Nixon's rhetoric reveals that the data reported here do not reflect inaugural rhetoric exclusively. After analyzing the twenty-eight speeches by Nixon mentioned earlier, speeches which contained references to the deity and speeches which were delivered in a wide variety of rhetorical settings, the following proportions were revealed: God the Inscrutable Potentate (37.7 percent of the references); God the Witnessing Author (19.6 percent); God the Wise and the Just (6.5 percent); God the Genial Philanthropist (28.0 percent); and God the Object of Affection (8.2 percent). Thus, except for Nixon's being a bit less taken with the wisdom and justice of the Lord, his overall rhetorical behavior is quite reminiscent of the inaugural remarks made by his predecessors in office.

11. Robert Alley has suggested that each of America's presidents has embraced a particular God, implying that the "pantheon" I am describing here is made up of a variegated grouping of individually prized gods. Says Alley: "When Americans determine to inject God into this political complexity in order to simplify by divine decree, the question is raised as to who is this God. Is he the selective God of judgment that inspired Wilson? Is he the God of business who rewards those who practice diligence as defined by Hoover? Is he the God of the universe whose benevolent plan may inspire all men as it did Roosevelt? Is he the friendly sovereign who has chosen America, blessed her, and given her a special mission as seen by Truman and Eisenhower?" (Alley, p. 81). While Alley's argument may be correct, it should be noted that the data presented above do *not* support his contention as regards presidential inaugurals. Rather, most American presidents sampled liberally from the pantheon when framing their maiden remarks as chief executives.

12. Will Herberg, *Protestant, Catholic and Jew*, p. 285.

13. Annemarie de Waal Malefijt, *Religion and Culture*, p. 215.

14. Herberg, p. 285.

15. "Civil Religion *vs.* Biblical Religion," reprinted in *The Christian Patriot*, May 1973, pp. 6-7.

16. "The Church of the Covenants: Plans for the Bicentennial," *Bicentennial Broadside*, p. 30.

17. Ibid.

18. Lynn E. May, *Baptists and the Bicentennial* (pamphlet prepared by the Southern Baptist Council Historical Commission, 1975).

19. *Forward* 1 (Spring 1974): p. 4. (*Forward* is a periodical issued by the Interchurch Center in New York City.)

20. Willmoore Kendall and George W. Carrey, *The Basic Symbols of the American Political Tradition*, p. 12.

21. *The Word "Comrade," Should We Abandon it?*, (a publication of the Americanism Department, Veterans of Foreign War, n.d.), p. 2.

22. Ibid.

23. Joseph Costanzo, *This Nation Under God*, p. 34.

24. Leo Pfeffer, *Church, State, and Freedom*, p. 151.

25. See J. L. Austin, *How to Do Things with Words*.

26. *Time*, 13 November 1972.

27. Conrad Cherry, "American Sacred Ceremonies," in *American Mosaic: Social Patterns of Religion in the United States*, ed. Phillip E. Hammond and Benton Johnson (New York: Random House, 1970), p. 313.

28. Wallace Fisher, *Politics, Poker, and Piety*, p. 138.

29. Fox, p. 276. Things get a bit more confusing, of course, when civil war splits a nation (and its legitimizing God) apart. Rhetorically speaking, such an exigence requires that God take everybody's part. For an interesting discussion of such matters, see H. V. Taylor's study, "Preaching on Slavery, 1831-1861," in *Preaching in American History*, ed. D. Holland (New York: Abingdon Press, 1969), 168-83.

30. Andrew Greeley, *The Denominational Society*, p. 163.

31. Robert N. Bellah, "American Civil Religion in the 1970's," *Anglican Theological Review*, no. 1 (July 1973): 18-19.

32. Peter Berger, *The Sacred Canopy*, p. 32.

33. "Piety along the Potomac," *The Reporter*, 17 August 1954, p. 26.

34. (New York: The Christophers, 1964).

35. *To the Republic: One Nation under God* (South Bend, Ind.: Manion Forum, 1968), p. 4.

36. Malefijt, *Religion and Culture*, p. 162. Elsewhere, I have suggested that placing a rhetorical emphasis on the past is characteristic of much "true believer" discourse. While civil-religious discourse does not qualify for "true believer" status, the parallels are dramatic and worth noting. See "The Rhetoric of the True Believer," *Speech Monographs* 38 (November 1971): 249-61.

37. Vol. 46 (July-August 1973): 7.

38. "Religion and the 'Informing' of Culture," in *Religion's Influence in Contemporary Society*, ed. Joseph E. Faulkner (Columbus: Merrill, 1972), p. 282.

39. "This Nation Shall Endure," Address delivered at Brigham Young University, 4 December 1973, unpublished text, p. 8.

40. See M. Darroll Bryant, "America as God's Kingdom," in Jurgen Moltmann et al., eds., *Religion and Political Society* (New York: Harper, 1974), pp. 54-94.

41. Sidney Ahlstrom, *A Religious History of the American People*, p. 311.

42. J. F. Maclear, "The Republic and the Millenium," in *Religion of the Republic*, ed. Elwyn A. Smith (Philadelphia: Fortress Press, 1971), 183-216.

43. Mentioned in *The Light in the Steeple* (New York: National Council of Churches, 1975), p. 8.

344. Maclear, p. 204. See also William Gribbin, *The Churches Militant*, p. 130.

45. See Ray Abrams, *Preachers Present Arms*.

46. Quoted in Alley, p. 80.

47. "Resignation Address," *New York Times*, 16 October 1973, p. 34.

48. Personal communication, 22 January 1974. Rev. Litfin is an assistant professor of practical theology at Dallas Theological Seminary, Dallas, Texas.

49. Thomas O'Dea, *Sociology and the Study of Religion*, p. 242.

50. *The Catholic War Veteran*, July-August 1973, p. 5.

51. Ibid.

52. Conrad Cherry, "Two American Sacred Ceremonies: Their Implications for the Study of Religion in America," *American Quarterly*, vol. 21, no. 4, Winter, 1969, p. 754.

53. Paul Blanshard, *God and Man in Washington,* p. 3.
54. Clarence DiChiara, "National 1st Vice Commander's Program for 1973-1974," (unpublished memorandum of the American Legion, October 1973), p. 3.
55. Fox, pp. 263-64.
56. Ibid., p. 263.
57. Costanzo, p. 35.
58. Michael Novak, *Choosing our King,* p. 3.
59. Ibid., p. 193.
60. For a more complete understanding of this particular service, see Ben Hibbs, ed., *White House Sermons* (New York: Harper, 1972), pp. 62-69.
61. Edward B. Fiske, "Controversy over those White House Services," *New York Times,* 10 August 1969, p. 7.
62. Bellah, "Civil Religion in America," p. 15.
63. Ibid., p. 5.
64. If asked, Irving Kristol would probably agree with the position being taken here—that *rhetorical conventions,* not philosophical predilections, are the operant forces in much presidential discourse. Says Kristol: "Some time around the turn of the century, the impact of the Populist and Progressive movements combined to establish the vernacular utopian-prophetic rhetoric as the official rhetoric of American statesmen. It happened gradually, and it was not until the nineteen-thirties that the victory of the vernacular was complete and unchallengeable. But it also happened with a kind of irresistible momentum, as the egalitarian, 'democratic' temper of the American people remorselessly destroyed the last vestiges of the neo-Whiggish, 'republican' cast of mind. By now, we no longer find it in any way odd that American Presidents should sound like demagogic journalists of yesteryear. Indeed, we would take alarm and regard them as eccentric if they sounded like anything else." See *On the Democratic Idea in America,* p. 134.
65. Winthrop Hudson, *Religion in America,* p. 112.
66. Bernard Bailyn, *The Ideological Origins of the American Revolution,* p. 251.
67. Richard K. Fenn, "Toward a New Sociology of Religion," *Journal for the Scientific Study of Religion* 11, no. 1 (March 1972): 21.
68. *Service to God and Country Handbook* (Indianapolis: The American Legion, 1971), p. 3.
69. Murray Edelman, *The Symbolic Uses of Politics,* p. 125.
70. Cherry, "American Sacred Ceremonies," p. 311. Lloyd Warner views America's holidays as performing the same sort of unifying function we are noting here. See his *American Life.*
71. Martin E. Marty, Stuart E. Rosenberg and Andrew M. Greeley, *What Do We Believe?* (New York: Meredith, 1968), p. 28.
72. Quoted in Abrams, p. 121.
73. "How to Improve your Government: 19 Tips," *Christopher News Notes,* no. 138, October 1964, not paginated.
74. Cherry, "Two Sacred Ceremonies," p. 742.

75. "The Election Sermon: Primer for Revolutionaries," *Speech Monographs* 29, no. 1 (March 1962): 22.

76. "The Fact of Pluralism and the Persistence of Sectarianism," in *Religion of the Republic*, ed. Elwyn A. Smith (Philadelphia: Fortress Press, 1971), pp. 251-52.

77. Andrew M. Greeley, *Unsecular Man*, p. 93.

78. Conrad Cherry, *God's New Israel*, p. 18. Kenneth Burke, especially, sees mythification to be essential to all political orders. Such myths, implies Burke, allow governments to transcend the mundane and groveling imprecations of feckless nationalism in favor of a more majestic view of the collective's destiny. See his *A Rhetoric of Motives*, pp. 113-14.

79. Kristol, pp. 148-49.

80. Anecdotally, at least, Kristol's assumption seems to hold when the rhetoric of America's statesmen is compared to that of Great Britain's leaders: "'If you desire a purpose in life,' Prime Minister Heath told some of his idealistic constituents, 'don't come to me. Kindly call on your archbishop.'" Quoted in Novak, p. 108.

81. Abrams, pp. xvii-xviii.

82. Quoted in Peter L. Berger and Daniel Pinard, "Military Religion: An Analysis of Educational Materials Disseminated by Chaplains," in *Military Chaplains: From a Religious Military to a Military Religion*, ed. Harvey G. Cox (New York: American Report Press, 1971), p. 92.

83. David O. Moberg, *The Church as a Social Institution*, p. 161.

84. William L. Miller, *Piety Along the Potomac* (New York: Houghton, 1964), p. 41.

85. Robert D. Clark, "The Oratorical Career of Bishop Matthew Simpson," *Speech Monographs* 16, no. 1 (1949): 4.

86. *Protestant, Catholic and Jew*, p. 96.

87. William L. Miller, "American Religion and American Political Attitudes," in *Religious Perspectives in American Culture*, ed. James W. Smith and A. Leland Jamison (Princeton: Princeton University Press, 1961), p. 93.

88. Paul Blanshard, *God and Man in Washington*, p. 21.

89. Hudson, p. 114.

90. Quoted in the *National Catholic Reporter*, vol. 10, 23 November 1973, p. 4.

91. *Dwight D. Eisenhower: In Memoriam* (pamphlet issued by the Billy Graham Evangelistic Association, 1969), not paginated.

92. George H. Williams, "The Chaplaincy in the Armed Forces of the United States of America in Historical and Ecclesiastical Perspective," in *Military Chaplains: From a Religious Military to a Military Religion*, ed. Harvey G. Cox (New York: American Report Press, 1971), p. 14.

93. Mary Ruth Cavanaugh, "The Ladies' Auxiliary's National President's Message," *Catholic War Veteran*, January-February 1974, p. 7.

94. Herbert Schneider, *Religion in Twentieth Century America*, p. 32.

95. John F. Wilson, "The Status of 'Civil Religion' in America," in *The Religion of the Republic,* ed. Elwyn A. Smith (Philadelphia: Fortress Press, 1971), p. 5. Felix Keesing has suggested that religion-in-general is possessed of special emotional resources during anxious times. See his *Cultural Anthropology,* pp. 328-29.

96. *Protestant, Catholic and Jew,* p. 97.

97. Sperry, p. 252.

98. "This Nation Shall Endure," an address delivered at Brigham Young University in Provo, Utah, on 4 December 1973.

99. Ibid.

100. "I Pledge Allegiance," in *Creative Help for Daily Living* 25 (July 1974): p. 9.

101. Blanshard, p. 33.

102. Robert E. Fitch, "Piety and Politics in President Eisenhower," *The Antioch Review* 15, no. 2 (Summer 1955): 154.

103. Bellah, "Civil Religion in America," p. 18.

104. Robert M. Bellah, *The Borken Covenant,* p. 162.

105. "In God Let us Trust," in H. D. Moore, E. A. Ham, and C. E. Hobgood (eds.), *And Our Defense is Sure* (New York: Abingdon, 1964), p. 152.

Postlude

1. William Gribbin, *The Churches Militant,* p. 19.

2. Quoted in Paul Blanshard, *God and Man in Washington,* p. 32.

3. See Richard K. Fenn, "Toward a New Sociology of Religion," *Journal for the Scientific Study of Religion* 11, no. 1 (March 1972): 16-32.

4. Conrad Cherry, *God's New Israel,* p. 19.

5. Ernest S. Bates, *American Faith,* p. 86.

SELECTED BIBLIOGRAPHY

Included here are commentaries of both a scholarly and a popular nature. Excluded are references to actual pieces of discourse, a decision mandated by the sheer enormity and bewildering diversity of the rhetoric investigated in this essay.

Books

Abrams, Ray. *Preachers Present Arms.* New York: Round Table Press, 1933.

Ahlstrom, Sidney E. *A Religious History of the American People.* New Haven: Yale University Press, 1972.

Alley, Robert S. *So Help Me God: Religion and the Presidency.* Richmond, Va.: John Knox Press, 1972.

Austin, J. L. *How To Do Things With Words.* New York: Oxford University Press, 1965.

Bailyn, Bernard. *The Ideological Origins of the American Revolution.* Cambridge, Mass.: Harvard University Press, 1967.

Bates, Ernest S. *American Faith.* New York: Norton, 1940.

Bell, Bernard I. *Crowd Culture.* New York: Harper, 1952.

Bellah, Robert N. *Beyond Belief: Essays on Religion in a Post-Traditional World.* New York: Harper & Row, 1970.

———. *The Broken Covenant: American Civil Religion in Time of Trial.* New York: Seabury Press, 1975.

Berger, Peter L. *The Noise of Solemn Assemblies.* Garden City, N.Y.: Doubleday & Co., 1961.

———. *The Sacred Canopy.* Garden City, N.Y.: Doubleday & Co., 1967.

Beth, Loren. *The American Theory of Church and State.* Gainesville: University of Florida Press, 1958.

Blanshard, Paul. *God and Man in Washington.* Boston: Beacon Press, 1960.

Burke, Kenneth. *A Rhetoric of Motives.* Berkeley: University of California Press, 1969.
_____. *Attitudes Toward History.* Vol. 1. New York: New Republic, 1937.
_____. *Language as Symbolic Action: Essays on Life, Literature, and Method.* Berkeley: University of California Press, 1968.
Campbell, Colin. *Toward a Sociology of Irreligion.* New York: Macmillan Co., 1971.
Cherry, Conrad. *God's New Israel: Religious Interpretations of American Destiny.* Englewood Cliffs, N. J.: Prentice-Hall, 1971.
Cherry, Conrad, and Fenton, John Y., eds. *Religion in the Public Domain.* University Park: Pennsylvania State University Press, 1966.
Clancy, William, et al. *Religion and American Society.* Santa Barbara, Calif.: Center for the Study of Democratic Institutions, 1961.
Costanzo, Joseph F. *This Nation Under God.* New York: Herder & Herder, 1964.
Cousins, Norman, ed. *In God We Trust: The Religious Beliefs and Ideas of the Founding Fathers.* New York: Harper & Row, 1958.
Cutler, Donald R., ed. *The Religous Situation: 1968.* Boston: Beacon Press, 1968.
Duncan, Hugh. *Communication and Social Order.* New York: Bedminster Press, 1962.
Eddy, Sherwood. *The Kingdom of God and the American Dream.* New York: Harper & Row, 1941.
Edelman, Murray. *The Symbolic Uses of Politics.* Champaign: University of Illinois Press, 1964.
Fisher, Wallace E. *Politics, Poker, and Piety.* Nashville, Tenn.: Abingdon Press, 1972.
Gaustad, Edwin S. *A Religious History of America.* New York: Harper & Row, 1966.
Glock, Charles Y., and Stark, Rodney. *Religion and Society in Tension.* Chicago: Rand McNally & Co., 1965.
Gordon, George N. *Persuasion: The Theory and Practice of Manipulative Communication.* New York: Hastings House, 1971.
Greeley, Andrew M. *The Denominational Society.* Glenview, Ill.: Scott, Foresman & Co., 1972.
_____. *Unsecular Man.* New York: Schocken Books, 1972.
Gribbin, William. *The Churches Militant.* New Haven: Yale University Press, 1973.
Handy, Robert T. *A Christian America.* New York: Oxford University Press, 1971.
Heimert, Alan. *Religion and the American Mind.* Cambridge, Mass.: Harvard University Press, 1966.
Henderson, Charles P. *The Nixon Theology.* New York: Harper & Row, 1972.
Herberg, Will. *Protestant, Catholic and Jew.* Garden City, N.Y.: Doubleday & Co., 1955.
Hudson, Winthrop. *Religion in America.* 2d ed. New York: Charles Scribner's Sons, 1973.

Jewett, Robert. *The Captain America Complex.* Philadelphia: Westminster Press, 1973.
Keesing, Felix M. *Cultural Anthropology.* New York: Holt, Rinehart, & Winston, 1965.
Kendall, Willmoore, and Carey, George W. *The Basic Symbols of the American Political Tradition.* Baton Rouge: Louisiana State University Press, 1970.
Kristol, Irving. *On the Democratic Idea in America.* New York: Harper & Row, 1972.
Littell, Franklin H. *From State Church to Pluralism.* Chicago: Aldine Publishing Company, 1962.
McAvoy, Thomas T., ed. *Roman Catholicism and the American Way of Life.* South Bend, Ind.: University of Notre Dame Press, 1960.
McNamara, Patrick H. *Religion American Style.* New York: Harper & Row, 1974.
McWilliams, Wilson C. *The Idea of Fraternity in America.* Berkeley: University of California Press, 1974.
Malefijt, Annemarie de Waal. *Religion and Culture.* New York: Macmillan Co., 1968.
Marty, Martin E. *The New Shape of American Religion.* New York: Harper & Row, 1958.
_____. *Righteous Empire.* New York: Dial Press, 1970.
Marty, Martin E., Rosenberg, Stuart E., and Greeley, Andrew M. *What Do We Believe?* New York: Meredith, 1968.
Mead, Sidney E. *The Lively Experiment.* New York: Harper & Row, 1963.
Miller, William L. *Piety Along the Potomac.* New York: Houghton Mifflin Co., 1964.
Moberg, David O. *The Church as a Social Institution.* Englewood Cliffs, N.J.: Prentice-Hall, 1962.
Morgan, Richard E. *The Politics of Religious Conflict.* Indianapolis: Pegasus, 1968.
Nichols, Roy I. *The Religion of American Democracy.* Baton Rouge: Louisiana State University Press, 1959.
Nottingham, Elizabeth K. *Religion: A Sociological View.* New York: Random House, 1971.
Novak, Michael. *Ascent of the Mountain, Flight of the Dove: An Invitation to Religious Studies.* New York: Harper & Row, 1971.
_____. *Choosing Our King.* New York: Macmillan Co., 1974.
O'Dea, Thomas F. *Sociology and the Study of Religion.* New York: Basic Books, 1970.
O'Hair, Madlyn Murray. *Freedom Under Seige.* Los Angeles: J. P. Tarcher, 1974.
Pfeffer, Leo. *Church, State, and Freedom.* Boston: Beacon Press, 1953.
Richey, Russell, and Jones, Donald, eds. *American Civil Religion.* New York: Harper & Row, 1974.
Salisbury, W. Seward. *Religion in American Culture.* Homewood, Ill.: Dorsey Press, 1964.
Schneider, Herbert W. *Religion in Twentieth Century America.* Cambridge, Mass.: Harvard University Press, 1952.

Smith, Elwyn A., ed. *The Religion of the Republic.* Philadelphia: Fortress Press, 1971.

Sperry, Willard L. *Religion in America.* Boston: Beacon Press, 1946.

Streiker, Lowell D., and Strober, Gerald S. *Religion and the New Majority.* New York: Association Press, 1972.

Strout, Cushing. *The New Heavens and the New Earth: Political Religion in America.* New York: Harper & Row, 1974.

Warner, W. Lloyd. *American Life.* Chicago: University of Chicago Press, 1953.

Weiss, Benjamin. *God in American History.* Grand Rapids, Mich.: Zondervan, 1966.

Wilson, John F., ed. *Church and State in American History.* Lexington, Mass.: D. C. Heath & Co., 1965.

Chapters, Articles, Pamphlets

Ahlstrom, Sydney E. "The American National Faith: Humane, Yet All Too Human." In *Religion and the Humanizing of Man*, edited by James M. Robinson. Ontario, Canada: Council on the Study of Religion, 1973.

Barrett, Harold. "John F. Kennedy Before the Greater Houston Ministerial Association." *Central States Speech Journal* (November 1964): 259-66.

Baskerville, Barnett. "The Cross and the Flag: Evangelists of the Far Right." In *The Rhetoric of Our Times*, edited by J. Jeffery Auer. New York: Meredith, 1969.

Bellah, Robert N. "American Civil Religion in the 1970's." *Anglican Theological Review*, no. 1 (July 1973): 8-20.

———. "Civil Religion in America." *Daedalus* (Winter 1967): 1-21.

Berger, Peter, and Pinard, Daniel. "Military Religion: An Analysis of Educational Materials Disseminated by Chaplains." In *Military Chaplains: From a Religious Military to a Military Religion*, edited by Harvey G. Cox. New York: American Report Press, 1971.

Bicentennial Broadside. New York: United Church Board for Homeland Ministries, 1975.

Bitzer, Lloyd F. "The Rhetorical Situation." *Philosophy and Rhetoric* 1 (January 1968): 1-14.

Bryant, M. Darroll. "America As God's Kingdom." In *Religion and Political Society*, edited by Jurgen Moltmann et al. New York: Harper & Row, 1974.

Cherry, Conrad. "American Sacred Ceremonies." In *American Mosaic: Social Patterns of Religion in the United States*, edited by Phillip E. Hammond and Benton Johnson. New York: Random House, 1970.

———. "Two American Sacred Ceremonies: Their Implications for the Study of Religion in America." *American Quarterly* 21, no. 4 (Winter 1969): 739-54.

Clark, Robert D. "The Oratorical Career of Bishop Matthew Simpson." *Speech Monographs* 16, no. 1 (1949): 1-20.

Cole, William A., and Hammond, Phillip E. "Religious Pluralism, Legal Development, and Societal Complexity: Rudimentary Forms of Civil Religion." *Journal for the Scientific Study of Religion* 13, no. 2 (June 1974): 177-89.

Easton, David, and Hess, Robert D. "The Child's Political World." *Midwest Journal of Political Science* 6 (August 1962): 229-46.

Eubank, Wayne C. "Benjamin Morgan Plamer's Thanksgiving Sermon, 1860." In *Antislavery and Disunion, 1858-1861: Studies in the Rhetoric of Conflict and Compromise,* edited by J. Jeffery Auer. New York: Harper & Row, 1963.

Fabian, Johannes. "Genres in an Emerging Tradition: An Anthropological Approach to Religious Communication." In *Changing Perspectives in the Scientific Study of Religion,* edited by Allen W. Eister. New York: John Wiley & Sons, 1974.

Fenn, Richard K. "Toward a New Sociology of Religion." *Journal for the Scientific Study of Religion* 11, no. 1 (March 1972): 16-32.

Fitch, Robert E. "Piety and Politics in President Eisenhower." *The Antioch Review* 15, no. 2 (Summer 1955): 148-58.

Fox, Frederick. "The National Day of Prayer." *Theology Today* 26, no. 3 (October 1972): 258-80.

Greeley, Andrew. "The Civil Religion of Ethnic Americans: the Viewpoint of a Catholic Sociologist." *Religious Education* (September-October 1975): 449-513.

Hammond, Philip E. "Religion and the 'Informing' of Culture." In *Religion's Influence in Contemporary Society,* edited by Joseph E. Faulkner. Columbus, Ohio: Charles E. Merrill, 1972.

Hart, Roderick P. "The Rhetoric of the True Believer." *Speech Monographs* 38 (November 1971): 249-61.

Herberg, Will. "Religion and Culture in Present-Day America." In *Roman Catholicism and the American Way of Life,* edited by Thomas T. McAvoy. South Bend, Ind.: University of Notre Dame Press, 1960.

————. "Religion in a Secularized Society: The New Shape of Religion in America." In *The Sociology of Religion: An Anthology,* edited by Richard D. Knudten. New York: Meredith, 1967.

————. "Religion in a Secularized Society: Some Aspects of America's Three-Religion Pluralism." In *Religion, Culture, and Society,* edited by Louis Schneider. New York: John Wiley & Sons, 1964.

Higginbotham, Don. "The Relevance of the American Revolution." *Anglican Theological Review,* no. 1 (July 1973): 21-37.

Holmes, Urban T., "Revivals are Un-American: A Recalling of America to its Pilgrimage." *Anglican Theological Review,* no. 1 (July 1973): 58-75.

Huegli, Albert G. "New Dimensions in Church-State Relations." In *Church and State Under God,* edited by Albert G. Huegli. St. Louis: Concordia, 1964.

Jamieson, Kathleen. "Generic Calcification: An Undiagnosed Rhetorical Malady." Paper presented at the annual convention of the Speech Communication Association, New York, December 1974.
_____. "Generic Constraints and the Rhetorical Situation." *Philosophy and Rhetoric* 6 (Summer 1973): 162-70.
Kerr, Harry P. "The Election Sermon: Primer for Revolutionaries." *Speech Monographs* 29, no. 1 (March 1962): 13-22.
_____. "Politics and Religion in Colonial Fast and Thanksgiving Sermons, 1763-1783." *Quarterly Journal of Speech* 46, no. 4 (December 1960): 372-82.
The Light in the Steeple. New York: National Council of Churches, 1975.
Long, Charles H. "A New Look at American Religion." *Anglican Theological Review*, no. 1 (July 1973): 117-25.
McGloughlin, William G. "How is America Religious?" In *Religion in America*, edited by William G. McGloughlin and Robert N. Bellah. New York: Houghton Mifflin Co., 1968.
Maclear, J. F. "The Republic and the Millenium." In *Religion of the Republic*, edited by Elwyn A. Smith. Philadelphia: Fortress Press, 1971.
Martin, Howard H. "The Fourth of July Oration." *Quarterly Journal of Speech* 44, no. 4 (December 1958): 393-401.
Marty, Martin E. "Alternative Approaches in Church-State Relations." In *Church and State Under God*, edited by Albert G. Huegli. St. Louis: Concordia, 1964.
_____. "Sects and Cults." *The Annals of the American Academy of Political and Social Science* 332 (November 1960): 125-34.
Mead, Sidney E. "The Fact of Pluralism and the Persistence of Sectarianism." In *Religion of the Republic*, edited by Elwyn A. Smith. Philadelphia: Fortress Press, 1971.
Miller, William L. "American Religion and American Political Attitudes." In *Religious Perspectives in American Culture*, edited by James W. Smith and A. Leland Jamison. Princeton, N.J.: Princeton University Press, 1961.
Neuhaus, Richard J. "The War, the Churches, and Civil Religion." *The Annals* 387 (January 1970): 128-40.
Niebuhr, Reinhold. "The King's Chapel and the King's Court." *Christianity and Crisis*, 4 August 1969, pp. 211-12.
Pfeffer, Leo. "The Case for Separation." In *Religion in America*, edited by John Cogley. New York: Meridian, 1958.
_____. "Religion and the State." In *Religion, Culture, and Society*, edited by Louis Schneider. New York: Wiley, 1964.
Simons, Herbert. "The Carrot and Stick as Handmaidens of Persuasion in Conflict Situations." In *Perspectives on Communication in Social Conflict*, edited by Gerald R. Miller and Herbert W. Simons. Englewood Cliffs, N.J.: Prentice-Hall, 1974.
Smylie, James H. "Protestant Clergy, the First Amendment, and the Beginnings of a Constitutional Debate, 1781-1791." In *Religion of the Republic*, edited by Elwyn A. Smith. Philadelphia: Fortress Press, 1971.

Stauffer, Robert E. "Civil Religion, Technocracy, and the Private Sphere: Further Comments on Cultural Integration in Advanced Societies." *Journal for the Scientific Study of Religion* 12, no. 4 (December 1973): 415-25.

Stewart, Charles. "Separation of Church and State." In *Preaching in American History*, edited by Dewitte Holland. Nashville, Tenn.: Abingdon Press, 1969.

Taylor, H. V. "Preaching on Slavery, 1831-1861." In *Preaching in American History*, edited by Dewitte Holland. Nashville, Tenn.: Abingdon Press, 1969.

Thomas, Michael C. and Flippen, Charles C. "American Civil Religion: An Empirical Study." *Social Forces* 6 (December 1972): 218-25.

Thomas, J. Earl. "The Reform of the Racist Religion of the Republic." In *Religion of the Republic,* edited by Elwyn A. Smith. Philadelphia: Fortress Press, 1971.

Weigel, Gustave. "The Present Embarrassment of the Church." In *Religion in America,* edited by John Cogley. New York: Meridian, 1958.

Williams, George H. "The Chaplaincy in the Armed Forces of the United States of America in Historical and Ecclesiastical Perspective." In *Military Chaplains: From a Religious Military to a Military Religion,* edited by Harvey G. Cox. New York: American Report Press, 1971.

Wilson, John F. "The Status of 'Civil Religion' in America." In *The Religion of the Republic,* edited by Elwyn A. Smith. Philadelphia: Fortress Press, 1971.

Wolfarth, Donald L. "John F. Kennedy in the Tradition of Inaugural Speeches." *Quarterly Journal of Speech* 47, no. 2 (April 1961): 124-32.

Zahn, Gordon C. "Sociological Impressions of the Chaplaincy." In *Military Chaplains: From a Religious Military to a Military Religion,* edited by Harvey G. Cox. New York: American Report Press, 1971.

INDEX